Keynes P8

247023

CASTLES IN THE AIR

OTHER BOOKS BY LEONARD E. READ

Romance of Reality (o.p.)
Pattern for Revolt
Instead of Violence
Outlook for Freedom (o.p.)
Government: An Ideal Concept
   Governo Um Concito Ideal
Why Not Try Freedom?
   ¿Por Que No Ensayar la Libertad?
Elements of Libertarian Leadership
Anything That's Peaceful
   Todo Por la Paz
The Free Market and Its Enemy
   El Enemigo del Mercado Libre
Deeper Than You Think
Accent on the Right
The Coming Aristocracy
Let Freedom Reign
Talking to Myself
Then Truth Will Out
To Free or Freeze
Who's Listening?
Having My Way

LEONARD E. READ

CASTLES IN THE AIR

The Foundation for Economic Education, Inc.
Irvington-on-Hudson, New York 10533
1975

THE AUTHOR AND PUBLISHER

Leonard E. Read has been president of The Foundation for Economic Education since it was organized in 1946.

The Foundation is a nonpolitical, nonprofit, educational institution. Its senior staff and numerous writers are students as well as teachers of the free market, private ownership, limited government rationale. Sample copies of the Foundation's monthly study journal, *The Freeman,* are available on request.

Published March 1975

ISBN-0-910614-52-0

To our Founding Fathers
who put foundations under history's greatest castle in the air. May we find meaning in The Bicentennial by restoring those foundations.

How long will the Republic endure? So long as the ideas of its founders remain dominant.

David Starr Jordan, *President*
Stanford University—1891-1913

CONTENTS

vii

1

CASTLES IN THE AIR

If you have built castles in the air,
your work need not be lost; there
is where they should be. Now put
foundations under them.
            —HENRY DAVID THOREAU

Scrutinize tradition and assess it, for it bears witness both true and false; to be blindly guided by it is to risk being led astray. So, beware of conventional thinking; break with tradition whenever reason shows its folly! As Ortega warned:

The so-called Renaissance was, for the moment, the attempt to let go of the traditional culture which, formed during the Middle Ages, had begun to stiffen and to quench man's spontaneity . . . man must periodically shake himself free of his own culture.[1]

Thoreau was a hardheaded searcher for truth; he did his own thinking. His comment on castles in the air is a sample, a

---

[1]See *Man and Culture* by José Ortega y Gasset (New York: W. W. Norton & Company, Inc., 1962), pp. 72-73.

break with the conventional definition of daydreaming: "Anything imagined and desired but not likely to be realized."

Thoreau is right. Contrary to popular notions, castles in the air are the birthplaces of human evolution; all progress, (and all regress) be it material, intellectual, moral, or spiritual, involves a break with the prevailing ideology. Not to break with the current conventions—to go on our dizzy way—means a headlong plunge into all-out socialism!

Castles in the air might indeed become chambers of horror. On the other hand, they encompass man's unrealized goals and aspirations, the dreams not yet attained but not necessarily unattainable. An example from the past may help show their role for the future: In 1898 it was thought that intensive farming depended on the nitrate mines in Chile, and that their eventual exhaustion would bring world famine. Why did not this disaster come to pass? Three great scientists built castles in the air. *They put foundations under them* and thereby "solved the problem of nitrogen via ammonia synthesis from air and water."[2] Result? More intensive farming than ever before! So we are not now dependent on nitrate from communist Chile; we do not face famine.

As to the future, such normal sources of energy as coal and oil are believed to be in critical shortage. "Energy crisis" is the talk of our time. Thank heaven for castles in the air. It has been known for centuries that all heat, light, and energy for the entire solar system comes from the sun. Coal and oil are but by-products thereof, the secondary sources we have used to survive. Very well! Why not anticipate the end of coal and

---

[2]See "Energy: The Ultimate Raw Material" by James Wei (*The Freeman*, August, 1972).

oil and go directly to the sun for mankind's energy? Harness energy at its source! *Put foundations under it!* Long steps in that direction have been taken, and it's now only a matter of time—assuming some other castles in the air—before we will be capable of extracting more energy from the sun than human beings may ever need.[3]

Why the reservation, "assuming some other castles in the air"? It is this: If we persist in coming to be more and more like communist Chile, solar energy for mankind is a daydream without foundation. Tapping this source on a meaningful scale is out of the question except as there be at least one country in the world where men are free. Put this stark fact another way: Solar energy will not grace mankind unless we remove our restraints against the release of creative human energy; solar energy and creative human energy are inseparably linked!

Freedom does not make people strong; rather, it makes strength possible. It gives everyone an opening for intellectual, moral, and spiritual strength. With freedom, many will develop their faculties, some will not. The outcome depends on one's inner strength. Indeed, this inner strength occasionally shows forth in persons living under extreme authoritarianism.

While such rare stalwarts as a Solzhenitsyn may keep a few sparks aglow, it is only when freedom's flame is high and bright—when millions are free to act creatively—that such

---

[3]"Although less than half the earth's sunlight entering the earth's atmosphere reaches its surface, just 40 minutes of that solar input equals all the energy mankind consumes in an entire year." In a word, 13,140 times as much solar energy as needed to serve present requirements. See "Tapping the Sun's Energy" by David G. Lee *(National Wildlife,* August-September, 1974).

miracles as tapping solar energy are a possibility. The ones who get the credit—the scientists out front—actually ride on the shoulders of others with their thoughts, insights, intuitive flashes—countless thousands of unknown persons. For instance, did Johann Gutenberg invent the printing press? He is given the credit. The fact is that his was but a crowning achievement, a final touch to literally millions of antecedents —including the unknown hero who harnessed fire.

In view of the politico-economic trend in all nations toward all-out statism, any prospect for progress requires a turn-about in at least one nation. And the nation on which each of us must focus is his own. Only at home may one expect to put foundations under his dreams.

More than two centuries ago in this land of ours men built castles in the air. What was their dream? A country free from authoritarian tyranny; each citizen free to act creatively as he pleased, government limited to inhibiting destructive actions, invoking a common justice, keeping the peace! No political arrangement had ever matched this dream, even remotely. Castles in the air, indeed!

The challenge they faced was to *put foundations under their dreams!* And they did: The Declaration of Independence unseated government as the sovereign power and put the Creator there: ". . . all men are . . . endowed by their Creator with certain unalienable Rights, that among these are Life, Liberty. . . ."

The Declaration, however, was only the first stage in laying the greatest politico-economic foundation in the history of mankind. The next step—cementing the foundation—was the Constitution, further supported by the Bill of Rights. These political instruments held government to a more limited role than ever before. Result? The greatest outburst of creative energy ever known—the American miracle!

What has happened? Our foundations are crumbling. We are reverting to the same type of authoritarianism from which our forefathers fled. We give it new names: the planned economy, the welfare state, socialism, communism. But tyranny is tyranny whether the master be a King James, a feudal lord, a Hitler, or a majority gone mad!

The remedy? Once again, castles in the air! Required is a lodestar—"a guiding ideal"—similar to that of our founding fathers, along with the will and the understanding to put foundations under that ideal.

Built into this foundation structure are gems of thought. The mortar holding the gems in place is composed of the several virtues: steadfastness of purpose; thinking for self rather than imitating others; an insatiable desire to learn, realizing that the more one learns the more there is to learn; an ability to explain the fallacies of all dictatorial behavior; an understanding of and a devotion to the creative process; and, this above all, integrity—the accurate reflection in word and deed of whatever one's highest conscience dictates as righteous.

Given such a foundation, what sequence of events might be expected to follow? A repeal of all laws that restrain or prohibit creative activity. A precedent for such a wholesome turn of events occurred in England following the Napoleonic wars. Richard Cobden and John Bright and a few enthusiastic supporters who understood the folly of mercantilism and the merit of freedom in transactions began the greatest reform movement in British history: the wholesale repeal of restrictive laws. As a consequence, England stood as a giant among nations until just before World War I when her foundations began to crumble, as ours are now crumbling. However, what happened once to achieve freedom in England can happen again there and also here. It can happen if there is the will to prevail, a faith that we can succeed.

Given a return to freedom, what about the harnessing of solar energy? It will be as commonplace a few years hence as delivering the human voice around the earth at the speed of light is today. Taken for granted! And who knows what other things free men can and will accomplish!

But far more important than these countless material blessings will be a freeing of the human spirit—tens of millions no longer wards of government but growing, emerging, self-responsible citizens, each his own man. Castles in the air? Let us build foundations under those worth keeping.

*   *   *

The following chapters are all castles in the air. Let me explain.

Our goal is that of free men in a free society—as high as one can aim in the hierarchy of intellectual, moral, and spiritual values. There is no limit to the ideas involved, ranging from exposure of authoritarian fallacies to infinite speculations on what is right and true. It is a tremendous challenge.

The best anyone can do is to think through for himself whatever thoughts flash into his mind. The chapters that follow are recordings and explanations of several thoughts which have occurred to me during the past year.

So, I offer these—my castles in the air—to anyone who may be interested in building foundations.

2

FREEDOM: A NEW VISION

A system of fixed concepts is contrary to natural law. It prevents life from flowing. It blocks the passage of the universal law.
—NEWTON DILLAWAY

Most of us who stand for the free society become exasperated, even angry, at our opponents. This reaction is almost instinctive, but I am convinced that it is a mistake. Actually, if any exasperation is warranted, it might better be directed at ourselves. Why this claim?

Assuming freedom to be the true and right way, which I do, those folks on the other side of the fence play a part, no less important than ourselves, in its attainment. Again, why? The vision of truth, the evolution of man, all progress—material, intellectual, moral, spiritual—is the result of action and reaction. Emerson called it "the law of compensation . . . no man thoroughly understands a truth until first he has contended against it." A self-evident fact: It is impossible to move forward unless there be something to thrust against.

View our opponents as welcome springboards—be grateful for their existence. "He that wrestles with us strengthens our nerves and sharpens our skill," wrote Edmund Burke. "Our antagonist is our helper."

Our philosophical and ideological adversaries are doing their part. Sometimes, indeed, it appears that they may take over. Their *action* is well nigh overwhelming, so enormous is its scale! It is our *reactions* that are faulty. For the most part, we react in the form of name-calling, disdain, often bitterness. How should we react? What is the intelligent way? We should use their notions as springboards to make our own case. If our reactions were adequate, they would cause freedom to appear as a brilliant star in the darkness—all eyes attracted to it. What follows is but another attempt on my part to light a candle—my *reactions* to prevailing conditions.

Reverting to the title: why speak of freedom as a vision? Freedom, as I shall define it, is but another castle in the air, an ideal way of life more ardently to be hoped for than seriously expected in our time. Sometime in the future, of course, but not right now!

And why the adjective "new"? To refute our opponents who continually refer to this way of life as "old hat" or words to that effect! Troubles in society, brought on by authoritarian mischief, they lay to freedom—quite innocently in most cases and for the reason that they have no understanding of what is meant by freedom in its higher sense. But let us be charitable; how many on our side of the fence have been or are clear in their own minds about freedom, and manifest it in their *actions?*

The truth is that freedom as it has been approximated, first in England and then in the U.S.A., is the newest and most remarkable politico-economic achievement in the world's history—enjoyed for five or six generations at most. The structures for this free way of life were erected in 1776: the simultaneous appearance of Adam Smith's *The Wealth of Nations* and the Declaration of Independence. It took a generation or two before these enlightenments brought forth their best fruit.

The issue is between two opposed ways of life. Our opponents' way is the older, as old as mankind: authoritarianism in its numerous forms, featuring fixed concepts which—as Dillaway points out—are contrary to natural law and prevent life from flowing. The newer is freedom, featuring unfixed, improving, flowing, creative concepts.

Anyone who believes as I do that man's earthly purpose is growth in awareness, perception, consciousness, has no choice but to side with individual liberty—freedom—and to look with disfavor on all forms of authoritarianism.[1]

Authoritarians at best can turn out carbon copies, no copy ever being as perfect as the imperfect original. Carbon copies cannot be improvements but only second-rate duplicates.

Human improvement or growth stems from an exercise of the faculties. This is no less true of the intellectual and spiritual than of the physical faculties. About your or my faculties and their potentialities no one else knows anything. Exercise is possible only as we are free to work on our individual selves and is diminished to the extent that we are worked over by others.

Growth without liberty, that is, without the freedom to ex-

---

[1]Most of what follows appears under the title, "The Miracle of the Market," one of six chapters in *Champions of Freedom* (Hillsdale, Michigan, Hillsdale College Press, 1974).

ercise our faculties and to discover our creative potentialities, is out of the question. Given the goal of individual
growth, authoritarianism is an utterly absurd way of life.

As perhaps anyone will readily surmise, I am addressing
myself to an ideal, the kind of a relationship between the
individual and society that has never existed. Why? Perfection can never be the product of imperfect man; at best the
ideal can only be approximated.

Why write about an impossible ideal? Unless we have the
ideal in our minds, we have no compass, no way of knowing
in which direction our efforts should be pointed. Knowing the
ideal is the first step in down-to-earth practicality.

I define the ideal—freedom in a refined state—as no man-
concocted restraints against the release of creative human
energy.

At The Foundation for Economic Education, my associates
and I refer to this ideal way of life as the freedom philosophy
—its practice an aspiration. In the economic realm we call it
the free market.

I have written over and over again that no one has more
than scratched the surface when it comes to understanding
and explaining the miracle of the market. And I can do no
more than make another scratch myself. Why? It is rather
difficult to explain a situation that has not existed. I must confine myself to hypothesizing.

Not at all surprisingly, most people think of the free market
as private enterprise. This, however, is not what we mean. All
sorts of wholly objectionable enterprises are private: piracy,
for instance, or embezzlement, hi-jacking. Nor are there many
business firms in America that are free market examples.
Labor union tactics are linked with many of them or, if not

this, there are governmental interventions that favor some and injure others

The free market is so little trusted because so few are aware of what it is. Thinking of ourselves as if we were a free people leads us mistakenly to conclude that our present hodge-podge of intervention is a manifestation of the free market. Consequently, we imagine that a free and self-responsible people would behave no better than do the majority of us today. But what we mean and what most people think we mean are poles apart!

In brief, the freedom philosophy or the free market is a way of life. But it differs from most philosophies in that it does not prescribe how any individual should live his life; there are no fixed concepts. It allows freedom for each to do as he pleases —live in accord with his own uniqueness as he sees it—so long as the rights of others are not infringed, which is to say, so long as no one does anything which were everyone to do would bring all of us to grief or ruin. In short, this way of life commends no controls external to the individual beyond those which a government limited to keeping the peace and invoking a common justice might impose. Each individual acts on his own authority and responsibility. Those incapable of self-support, instead of becoming wards of the state, may rely upon the charitable instincts and practices of a free people—a quality of character that thrives only when a people are free, when the fruits of their labors are theirs to do with as they see fit.

This is all there is to my definition; it is so brief because it is not prescriptive—no fixed concepts. It has nothing in it at all that calls on me or the government to run your life.

At this point I would like to comment on the danger of

labeling the ideal. There was a word that I always liked; the classical economists used it: liberal. The word liberal really meant, in the classical sense, the liberalization of the individuals from the tyranny of the State. That word was expropriated by our opponents and it has now come to mean liberality with other people's money. The word was taken over. And so I, more than anybody else, was responsible for introducing and publicizing and perhaps making world-wide the word libertarian. I am sorry I ever did it. Why? Because the word libertarian has now been just as much expropriated as the word liberal. Some years ago, after popularizing the word, I was at Stanford University where the Dean of the Graduate School of Business, Hugh Jackson, had a luncheon for me with his faculty. They were criticizing me for popularizing the word libertarian. And finally in desperation I said, "Well, what's wrong with it?" And somebody said it sounds too much like libertine. My rebuttal was, "I suppose you guys wouldn't eat horehound candy!" I do not use the word libertarian anymore, simply because if somebody said to me, Read, what is your position, and I say libertarian, they'll identify me with everyone from a socialist to an anarchist. Now, when they ask me where I stand, my answer is: I have an ideal in mind. At this point a dialogue is likely to begin and I might learn more from the other fellow than he from me. I do not wish to put any label on the ideal.

Reflect on the light spectrum. Political-economic philosophy also spreads over a wide spectrum and is loosely analogous to the light spectrum: red at the left produced by the longer wave lengths—the easiest observed—extending with ever shorter wave lengths through orange, yellow, green, blue, and finally to violet—the least discernible by the human eye. Colorblind people can often see red but their discernment decreases as the wave lengths shorten; many people with "good" eyesight cannot discern violet.

Reverting to the politico-economic spectrum, let us substitute the long and short arms of government for the long and short wave lengths. At the extreme left we observe the long arm of government reaching into nearly every phase of human existence—authoritarianism, full force! Everybody can see this, and even feel it. Then as we move to the right on this spectrum, the arms of government become shorter, reaching into fewer and fewer facets of life. Finally, and comparable to the ultra violet lying just beyond the visible spectrum—were such an ideal situation ever to exist—we would find the arms of government so short that they could not reach into and have control over a single creative activity—government no more than a peace-keeping arm of society. This ideal can only be imagined for it has never existed and probably never will. It is nebulous as a dream and lacks the quality of specificity. The question is, should we try to label this ideal? Or, more particularly, its seekers or votaries?

It is, of course, appropriate to label the extreme left, for it is composed of hard stuff: brute force. We call it communism, socialism, fascism, and so on. It is a masterminding scheme, the parts of which can be seen as can a blueprint. It is a discrete politico-economic mechanism and specific to the core. This is definitely nameable, as is a constitution, or any document, or thing, or person.

As we move to the right on this spectrum, the schematic phase gradually lessens; the arms of government are shorter. Yet, we quite properly ascribe names to each of these, labels ranging all the way from liberal to conservative.

The concern here is with the ideal that lies beyond the right end of the visible spectrum where schemes to manage the lives of others would be nonexistent—the imaginable only. I say, call it the ideal and let it go at that!

Before going further, let's examine the millions who lord it over others—parents over children and vice versa, husbands over wives and vice versa, employees over employers and vice versa, politicians over citizens and vice versa. How are we to account for those afflicted with the authoritarian syndrome? What lies at the root of this egomania? From whence comes this dictatorial penchant?

Some insist that it is a natural, instinctive trait of the human being; others say it is rooted in fear. To Hobbes, men were brutes so life degenerated into a perpetual condition of "war against every other" in a struggle not just to survive but to dominate his fellows. President Wilson pressed for self-determination as a right of all people, on the assumption that they wanted to rule themselves. According to Hobbes, they want to rule each other. Even the distinguished moral philosopher, Adam Smith, suggests that this lust for power may be the principal motive for slavery: Said he, "The pride of man makes him love to domineer. . . ."

I am convinced that what we call a lust for power does not stem from any of these "causes" but, basically, from unawareness. It is a weakness more than a lust; men resort to force for a very simple and an easily observable reason: *they do not know any better*! With notable exceptions, men are:

- *unaware* of how little they know. Without an awareness of minuscule knowledge, they can envision a better world only as others are carbon copies of themselves. Their remedy? Cast others in their image by force, if neces-sary.

- *unaware* that were everyone identical all would perish!
- *unaware* that our infinite variation in talents and virtues merits approval rather than censure, for variation is im-plicit in the Cosmic Order.
- *unaware* of an inability to mold the life of another benefi-cially. Each individual has but the dimmest notion of his own miraculous being; about others he knows substan-tially nothing. Man is not the Creator!
- *unaware* that consciousness has its origin in the voice of the mind. This is composed of the voice within— reason, insights, and the like—plus those enlightened voices of others which one may perceive and embrace. Together, they make up and circumscribe one's con-sciousness.

As you see, I am insisting that the domineering trait has its origin in unawareness or, to put it bluntly, in sheer ignorance —whether evidenced by you or me or any others. To call it a natural instinct is to insult Nature! Or to argue that God does not know what he is up to!

Socrates was aware. He exclaimed, "I know nothing."

Montaigne was aware. He inscribed on his coat of arms, *"Que sais-je"?*—What do I know?

And the late Ludwig von Mises was aware, as he demon-strated during an evening at my Los Angeles home in 1941, shortly after his arrival in the U.S.A. Present were a dozen of the best friends of freedom in Southern California—Dr. Thomas Nixon Carver, Dr. Benjamin Anderson, Bill Mullen-dore, and the like. We listened to the great teacher for several hours. Finally, the President of the Chamber of Commerce said, "All of us will agree with you that we are headed for troubled times but, Dr. Mises, let's assume that you were the dictator of these United States and could impose any changes you think appropriate. What would you do?" Quick as a flash, Mises replied, "I would abdicate."

Now comes the difficult part, an attempt to explain how miraculous the free market could be if really trusted and used. There can be no precise blueprint for freedom. The ideal is hypothetical. But we have a great deal of solid evidence.

Here, at the outset, is the central, compelling fact, a truth that is almost unanimously overlooked: *the market possesses a wisdom that does not exist, even remotely, in any discrete individual.* For instance, because you cannot imagine how mail would be delivered ever so much more efficiently than now if turned over to the market, never, for heaven's sake, let your faith falter by reason of your infinitesimal know-how. To claim that the free market has a wisdom a million or billion times your own is a gross understatement.

I recall lecturing in Detroit in 1957. Present was K. T. Keller, Chrysler's President and one of the greatest production men of our country. Alfred Sloan was there, and other executives from General Motors—about a hundred of the most prestigious people in the automobile business. While addressing them, this thought came to me: "You know, we have seventy-five million automobiles in America today, and there is not a man on the face of the earth who knows how to make one." Well, K. T. Keller was startled and then confirmed that he himself did not know how to make an automobile.

Nearly two years later, in pursuing that point, I began a series of exercises—every day for six months. They are described in my *Elements of Libertarian Leadership*. The exercises are difficult and should not be attempted without a good measure of will power. They take five minutes a day; but if a day is missed, one must start over again. The exercise changes each month. The first month calls for contemplation of a different item each day—a piece of chalk, tomato, blade of grass, a pair of scissors, a cup, or whatever. The discipline is to concentrate on that item for five minutes and think of its various qualities. Try concentrating on anything for five minutes and watch your mind wander. Not easy! The item for this day was an ordinary wooden lead pencil. My questions: Cedar often is white so why is this wood pinkish? Is that lead? What is this coloring and what is the printing? Is that eraser rubber? On and on. At the conclusion of the exercise, I recalled the Detroit experience, and then this intriguing thought: Perhaps there is not a man on earth who knows how to make a thing as simple as a pencil!

The President of the world's largest pencil manufacturing company responded favorably to my request to visit his factory. A whole day there, observing the materials on the unloading platform: graphite, brass, wetting agents, lumber, and other items. I observed the extrusion process and all other phases of manufacture, and had an hour with the chemist. What is that? He would tell me. Then, what is that? As he went down each line of explanation, he would finally admit to not knowing. It seemed altogether appropriate to me to let a pencil write its own biography, "I, Pencil." Here is proof positive that no person knows how to make a simple wooden lead pencil. Yet, that year 1,600,000,000 pencils were made in the U.S.A. The piece has had world-wide distribution. No person questions the point. Anyone may have a copy for the asking.

In a word, why is it that you and I, as well as all others,

who know so little are able to obtain so much? From whence comes this enormous knowledge that does not remotely exist in any person?

Professor F. A. Hayek, one of the few known to me who glimpses this phenomenon, refers to it as knowledge in society. Edmund Burke called it an immemorial heritage. My favorite phrase is overall luminosity.

From a reading of Ortega's *What Is Philosophy?*, I inferred that philosophy is the art of going deep and bringing the findings to the surface in clarity. But if this were the case, then sooner or later every philosopher would wind up at the center—truth in its pristine purity! The answer to everything! That is not the way it works. It is just the opposite. It is not people going deep but, rather, going out into the infinite unknown. Instead of converging lines, they are diverging lines. One man goes out in search of truth and brings his find-

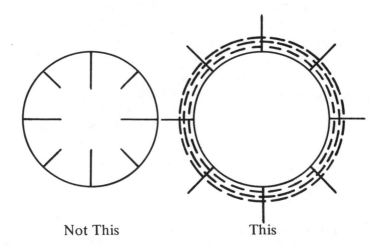

Not This   This

ing to the surface in clarity. This is what accounts for the overall luminosity. This is the wisdom by which we live. It does not exist in any discrete individual anywhere in the world, not even remotely.

If you wish proof, read *Treasury of Philosophy*[2]—about 1,000 pages. The book lists and describes the findings of four hundred of the world's most famous philosophers. It is interesting to note that no two of these men had the same experiences—no two of them alike! One man went out in one direction and found a bit of truth. Others went this way and that, bringing their varied findings back to the surface in clarity. This is the overall luminosity—the wisdom—by which we live. This explains the miracle of the market, a phenomenon that occurs when men are free. The full truth is not in you or me and never will be—nor in Socrates. But he had the distinct advantage of knowing he did not know!

Thinking of a philosopher as one who brings truth to the surface in clarity, nearly all individuals are philosophers to some extent. Millions upon millions over the millennia have brought one idea or more to the surface—have added to the luminosity by which we see, survive, and prosper.

What we must bear in mind is that the sole generative force at the human level stems from individual human faculties: intuition, insight, inventiveness, perception, awareness, consciousness, and the like. These qualities are present in all individuals—more or less.

Bear in mind that these qualities cannot be foreseen in another; indeed, not even in one's self. How can you foresee the original idea you may experience tomorrow!

---

[2]See *Treasury of Philosophy*, edited by Dagobert D. Runes (New York: The Philosophical Library, Inc., 1955).

An instructive event took place in Michigan during the last century. There was a little boy by the name of Tom, twelve years old—a newsboy on a train. One day the baggage man got so angry that he picked him up by the ears and threw him into the baggage car. The baggage man did not know that the waif he injured was Thomas Alva Edison. He did not know; you would not have known. Tom did not himself know what he would become. No one is aware of his potentialities! But look what happened to the lad Tom—he became the greatest inventive genius of all time.

To the extent that the free market prevails, to that extent is economic life featured by free entry and competition. Reflect on what this means. In addition to the heritage of the ages—the overall luminosity—these features enormously stimulate and bring to the fore the genius potentially existing among our contemporaries. Thus, it is possible for us to be graced not only by the accumulated knowledge and wisdom of the past but, also, by the considerably untapped ingenuity of the present. The best in everyone is brought forth when the best is required to succeed. The free market brings out the Edison in us!

The free market works its wonders simply because the generative capacity of countless millions has no external force standing against its release. Instead of preventing life from flowing, it permits life to flow! It is attuned to the natural, universal law.

Authoritarianism—regardless of the labels assigned to its numerous forms—presupposes nonexistent gods, that is, politicians who naively believe that they know how to steer mankind aright and, thus, can run your, my, and everyone else's life to humanity's advantage. These self-proclaimed wizards are in fact the most ignorant of all men. Why this derogatory assessment? They haven't taken the very first step in wisdom, namely, achieving an awareness of how little they know. While no wizard among them all can even make a pencil, each has little doubt that mankind, if made in his infinitesimal image, would be improved and that all of our millions of requirements would better prosper under his direction. Prosper? Preposterous!

The free market, on the other hand, is attuned to the little we know, it does not presuppose a nonexistent omniscience. Instead of trying vainly to make us into carbon copies of those who know not, the market relies upon man's immemorial heritage—the overall luminosity. This is where the needed knowledge waits to be drawn upon. Everyone's life is free to flow and grow—life's fulfillment a possibility for each human being. Admittedly, freedom in this higher sense is indeed a vision; it is a castle in the air under which we are well advised to put foundations.

My plea to each individual who has a faith in free men is to light a brighter candle than any of us, up till now, has been able to do. Growing, flowing is how we may approximate the vision.

3

THE MYSTERY
OF SOCIAL ORDER

> . . . she [order] is always to be
> found when sought for and never
> appears so lovely as when con-
> trasted with her opponent, dis-
> order.
>
> **—SAMUEL JOHNSON**

The word "order" has more than two dozen meanings, quite unrelated: order others to do this and that, money order, an order for government bonds, Order of the Double Dragon, and so on.

What I wish to examine here is an extremely critical kind of order—the social order that brings progress—as opposed to the disorder that is all too prevalent in today's world.

Most people seem to think of order as a fixed state in contrast to a condition of flux—everything neat, trim, definable, predictable—in a word, everything in its place and a place for everything. As related to the arrangement of things, this is commendable—in our homes and offices, for example. Many arrangements are sloppy, with all in confusion; no one can find anything. Others are models of organization, where things can be found with the eyes shut.

Think of a table setting—the knives, forks, spoons, dishes, napkins neatly in place for all persons. Now think of the goose step—the legs stiff and unbent, raised and lowered in unison by all persons.

But people are not things, and it is error of the first order to wish for fixed arrangements of people: *everyone in his place and a place for everyone!* Can it be that an accurate model of order as related to daily experiences with *things* provides a false model when it is a question of orderly human relations? Could it be that some such confusion underlies the current disintegration? The order desirable for things, when applied to persons, means the goose step literally and figuratively, and this is order's opponent, social disorder!

In the case of the goose step, what is the arrangement? Just this: a commander—"Do as I say, or else!"—and a corps of willing or subdued persons manipulated as automatons. Why do crowds so much admire this performance? Is it not the semblance of order that intrigues them? These same on-lookers wouldn't give a second glance at those soldiers were each free to go his own way. I have no objection to the goose step as entertainment, but is that kind of order appropriate for society?

What does the goose-step type of order presuppose above all else? A Hitler or his insane counterpart: how wondrous things would be were all mankind the likes of me! What else is presupposed? Millions of people who are willing to be manipulated as automatons, who like the notion of such a "shepherd," and even more millions who can be subdued by dictocratic power.

True, there is no large number of autocrats who would go all the way in imposing the goose-step type of order. However, there are untold millions today—politicians and bureaucrats—each with his own whimsical step which adds up to the same thing. Follow my order—on seat belts, wages, prices, interest rates, education, rationing, hours of labor, what and when to sow and reap, what and with whom exchanges may be made, what shall be used as money, on and on endlessly— do as I say! Anyone with the courage to look can see the goose step in these growing interventions—all contrived in the name of social order.

This is not to deny the role of government in maintaining social order—government limited to inhibiting the destructive actions of men: fraud, violence, stealing, predation, killing, misrepresentation; in a word, keeping the peace and invoking a common justice. Anarchy is no more viable than socialism; to practice either is to assure disorder.

Why is social order so mysterious? It is mysterious because no one can describe it in advance. Opposed to the perfect cadence of the goose step is the blessing that flows from everyone peacefully pursuing his own goals, going his way, that is, every which way, in constant flux, milling around, each person responding to his own ever-changing aspirations, abilities, uniqueness. Instead of our being carbon copies of some know-it-all, we are what we were meant to be: originals! Yet, these very differences appear as intolerable and disorderly to most people as things not in their place. They cannot imagine freedom as a means to social order.

Why can't we describe several billion originals in action? The reason is that no two among all who live on this earth are remotely identical. Each has gifts, aptitudes, and potentialities which distinguish him from everyone else. Not only is it impossible to describe these originals; there is not one among all of us who can come even close to describing his own undiscovered self. What thought, idea, invention, discovery, insight, intuitive flash will I experience this day or tomorrow or next year?

Bastiat wrote, "When goods do not cross borders, soldiers will." The sole reason that goods do not pass freely among people of all nations is that political goose steppers have interfered; they have impaired freedom in transactions. In this situation, international relations are governed by politicians from the several nations rather than by traders and their goods. The result? Friction, misunderstanding, ill will, soldiers crossing borders, arousing violent passions and *disorder.*

To grasp the full significance of Bastiat's observation, think of borders, not merely as the boundaries between nations or states or counties or towns, but as imaginary lines between you and me. To the extent that we are legally prevented from freely producing and exchanging with each other, to that extent will misunderstanding grow. Why? Simply because each of us is forced to behave as a carbon copy of assorted and countless dictocrats; we are images, not our real selves, no longer originals. Result: *disorder!*

Truly, social order is mysterious, yet it is possible for us to gain an awareness of its constitution. I concluded my comments on disorder by reference to a situation involving just the two of us. So I shall begin these comments on social order with the simplest form of "society"— you and me. Assume that we are now originals—no one else interfering with our production and exchange of goods and services. Freedom in transactions without let or hindrance! Observe how it works.

I have more corn than I can consume but want cattle. You have more cattle than you can feed so you want corn. I exchange some of my corn for a few of your cattle. Each of us gains. I thank you and you thank me. Why? The comforts of life are increased for both of us. You are a blessing to me and I to you. Good will abounds. There is harmony and order.

Finally, what is society but an enormous multiple of you's and me's? Discover what kind of behavior brings order for the two of us, and there is the correct formula for all of us.

Instead of only corn and cattle—the specializations of some —there are as many unique products as there are human beings, times all of the unique skills of each. To suggest that there are a trillion is to indulge in understatement. Who, in all the world, can comprehend, let alone manage, these! Such a thought is absurd.

So let all of us freely produce and exchange with our own countrymen or Frenchmen or Japanese or whom we please; and let us travel where we will. What is obviously appropriate for you and me is equally workable for all the human beings who inhabit this earth. All of us, here or there, near or far, exchanging our wares, *are the real ambassadors of good will and social order.* This would be a society of mutual benefit; or, we might say: The Thank You Society, under the Golden Rule.

4

PRICELESS—BUT NOT FREE

> *Liberty will not descend to a peo-*
> *ple; a people must raise them-*
> *selves to liberty;* it is a blessing
> that must be earned *before it can*
> *be enjoyed.*
>
> **—CALEB C. COLTON**

What is it that is priceless but not free? Human liberty! And
what is liberty? No restraints against the release of creative
energy! Liberty permits everyone to pursue his uniqueness,
that is, the open opportunity to grow, evolve, emerge, hatch.
If that is not a priceless situation—free to work toward human
destiny—pray tell, what is!

Next, why is liberty not free? In the case of early Americans, who were free, the responsibility for one's choice and
action—for his very life—was his own. It was root hog or die.
And they rooted. But once people experience the comfort and
affluence that are among the blessings of liberty, the link
between cause and consequence is not clear. There seems to
be more of a margin for error, a reserve against starvation,
an escape from self-responsibility, less need for liberty. This
however, is a dangerous illusion, for the price of liberty is

indeed eternal vigilance. In a condition of affluence, the requirement is to know one's self or perish. And we are perishing. Why? Self-examination is a price far beyond what most people are willing to pay, or to promise, or even to think about.

Perhaps to know one's self is not as difficult as first meets the eye. Certainly, we owe it to ourselves to try.

First, let us consider a little understood fact about our advanced industrial society. When each individual is free to pursue his uniqueness, no one produces exclusively for his own consumption; actually, in many instances, he consumes none of that which he produces. Rather, each does his "thing" while millions of others do their unique things, and the result is a miraculous abundance shared by all. For instance, I write and lecture about the freedom philosophy. In exchange for my small offerings others raise my food, build and repair my home, make my clothes, provide me with light and heat, cars and airplanes and so on. Reflect upon how I differ from my great-grandfather who, as an independent Jack-of-all-trades, was more or less self-sufficient. Americans today, myself included, have become dependent on each other—*interdependent*. A return to self-sufficiency is unthinkable.

Among the blessings of this interchange—interdependence —are comfort and affluence. But this very advanced way of life has a price tag. My ancestor was not obliged to get along with neighbors—he had none. His social problems? Almost nil! You and I? Millions are our neighbors. Social problems we have, indeed! No longer do we live as loners—we are now individualistic and social beings. And unless we learn effectively to be both at once, we perish. This is the dilemma we face.

The blessings of liberty Americans have had the privilege of sampling is something brand new in human experience. It cannot be said to antedate the appearance in 1776 of Adam Smith's *Wealth of Nations,* and of our own Constitution in 1789. As this new way of life progressed—featured as it is by specialization and division of labor—a new societal problem emerged: interdependence, an intimate interrelatedness that had not before challenged man's thinking. How to cope with it? What should, in this new situation, be the individual's attitude toward self and others? Think only of self, or solely of others, or what? These are the questions that have been plaguing us. The new and magnificent edifice tumbles into a shambles unless these matters are rightly resolved; unless we pay the price of coming to know ourselves, we perish.

Two opposing ways—both illogical in my view—have held and continue to hold the intellectual spotlight. One is founded on the notion that man is exclusively a social being, the other that he is only an individualistic being. One is known as altruism, the other as egotism. To pursue either way in a society of interdependent persons is to lose our way.

About a century after the free society began its emergence, the Frenchman, Auguste Comte, thought he had found the answer. Humanity was his god; his religion was that each one serves others: altruism. And it spread. A world of selfless persons, everyone thinking only of others and not at all of self! State socialism appears to be rooted in this concept. What other world could be less attractive—except a world of egotists?

Egotism is "self-conceit." The self, rather than humanity, is god. There is nothing in the universe over and beyond the egotist's mind, nor even any superior human being, past or present. The big I-Am does not conceive of himself in any respect as a social being—only individualistic. The foundation of anarchy!

Be it observed that each of us, despite pretensions to the contrary—even altruists and egotists—identifies with self-interest. We differ only in how intelligently we interpret what our self-interest is. Intelligence, in this respect, is the knowing of self. If I know myself not at all, thievery or legal plunder may seem to serve me best. However, if one truly knows the self—well, that's what I wish to explain.

In today's world, who are my neighbors? Only those who work, not for, but with me as if it were a pleasure? Only those who are on a first-name basis and live nearby? Actually, my neighbors are all over this world—millions of them, those who produce and exchange with me. Mostly, we have never heard of each other. I mention this fact to emphasize the extent to which we have become social beings, neighbors one and all. To know one's self requires a recognition of this brand new relationship, which is a product of liberty and the means to our survival.

Now to the final installment. At first blush this may seem somewhat esoteric, but think it through for yourself: *What I am has far more to do with what you are than is generally suspected.* To know one's self requires that the individual understand the role he is supposed to play. Each influences the rise or fall of society by what he is, how he acts, yes, even what his feelings are toward the millions on whom he is dependent. This is the way of life; otherwise, liberty wanes and we perish.

In this context, how should the key ingredient to knowing one's self be phrased? Reverence for life, all life, is my answer. While this trait is rare, it is possible for anyone to acquire.

Begin at the beginning with plant life. There is scientific evidence that plants fare far better in homes where they are loved than in homes where they are regarded indifferently. What goes on here? I suspect it is a form of radiation, a feeling that is of the heart, as we say; it is a quality that cannot be feigned. Plants are different by reason of what persons are.

Move on to bird life. A wild blue jay perches on the finger of my friend. Some people have a strange rapport with birds. While not common, numerous persons—more women than men—have achieved this form of radiation. Birds are different by reason of what persons are.

Move up the scale of life another step. Remember the motion picture, "Born Free," the true story of a lioness. What a different lioness by reason of that lady's reverence for life!

I have two shelties, remarkable for their affection. Why? Because that is what I accord them. Imagine how different they would be were I indifferent toward them. What I am has a great deal to do with what they are. My reverence for them is real, not feigned. Dogs, like other forms of life, can tell.

When it comes to the human level, reverence takes on another dimension: livelihood, the sustenance of life. In a word, we must revere or respect both life *and* livelihood. To impair livelihood, to deny ownership, is to take life, and it matters not whether this is done face-to-face or by legal plunder.

To repeat: What I am has far more to do with what you

are than is generally suspected. If I plunder others, their plundering tendencies are increased—tit for tat, an eye for an eye! If, on the other hand, I show a genuine reverence for life and livelihood, others will be inclined to accord the same, not only to me, but to one another as well.

As a famous physicist put it, every heartbeat is felt throughout the universe. Similarly, every thought of yours or mine, every act, all feelings—be they good or bad—are a form of radiation and this penetrates into the consciousness and behavior of our neighbors, the millions on whom you and I are dependent.

At the human level, the sole sources of good or evil are the you's and I's. If evil prevails, liberty wanes and we perish. But if each of us becomes an exemplar of moral and ethical principles, then liberty prevails and we prosper.

Not such an exorbitant price, after all, is it!

5

STRIVE FOR
THE SIMPLE LIFE

I love a life whose plot is simple.
—THOREAU

I, too, love a life whose plot is simple. However, my idea as to what's simple differs from that of the great naturalist and essayist, Henry David Thoreau. Doubtless, he had in mind the quietude of Walden Pond and its seclusion from society. And this is what nearly everyone regards as the simple life.

My great grandfather, born during the founding of America, was the first settler in Shiawassee County, Michigan. There was no "society" to interfere with his comings and goings—the nearest village being miles away—and except for the prying eyes of foraging Indians he and his family hacked it out alone. According to the popular definition, his life was indeed simple, far more so than Thoreau's.

What, really, *is* the simple life? Unless we settle that question, we will be plagued by a troublesome, socialistic cliche: "The more complex the society, the more government control we need." The result, eventually, will be out-

and-out dictatorship as intricacies in society are used as an excuse for total government. Is it not true that most people in today's world think of my great grandfather's life as simple and of mine as complex? Actually, it is the other way around. You and I really live the simple life, and this is the point I wish to clarify.

If, as I believe, man's purpose is to grow, evolve, emerge along the lines of his uniqueness, it follows that he must emerge from that poverty which attends those who are forced to become a Jack-of-all-trades. My great grandfather's unique talent might have been musical composition, or he might have become a distinguished naturalist and essayist, as did Thoreau—for all I know, or for all *he* knew! He, so preoccupied in doing nearly everything for himself, never had a chance to discover his uniqueness; he was imprisoned by the lack of opportunities to discover himself.

I reflected on the differences between my great grandfather's and my way of life on a recent flight from New York to Los Angeles. Think how complex it would have been for him to get from Shiawassee County to such a destination! Enormous preparations, hardships, and several months of dangerous travel! Me? Perfectly simple! All I did was to board a plane, debarking five hours later.

His wife had to weave and sew the clothes they wore— so complex a series of operations that only a very few in America today have any idea of how this is done. My case? My suit I had on was tailored in Hong Kong—12,000 miles away—the shirt in Madrid, the shoes in Rome. Complex? Indeed not; so simple that all I did was to sign three checks.

Came the luncheon at an altitude of 39,000 feet. Among the delectable dishes was fresh salmon from the Pacific

Northwest and broiled in the plane's kitchen. My part in this wonderful fare? As simple as waving a friendly greeting to a passing stranger! As to my ancestor, the complexities would have been too profound and numerous for him even to imagine. Salmon still fresh after 3,000 miles in transit! A jet plane never entered his head, or that broiler, or the coffee brewed from beans from another part of the world. My life is far more simple, much less complex, than his.

How explain this evolution toward civilization—from the complex to the simple life? How does one accomplish it? Instead of continuing as a recluse, leading a solitary, secluded existence, running away from others, man becomes civilized by getting into society, that is, by letting others with their unique talents come to one's aid. Let them do their countless things, which permits me to do my "thing." We need only remember that man is at once an individualistic and a social being, the latter no more warranting oversight than the former. Actually, the individualistic side of any person can never be fully realized except as the social side is understood, embraced, and skillfully exercised. Think of the things—literally millions of them—which are beyond your or my competence but by which you and I prosper.

Next, how shall this way of life in its ideal form be defined? I hesitate to use one apt expression, "social cooperation," for the reason that most statists, be they Russians or Americans, apply it to their coercive devices. Their command to "cooperate by doing as I say" is a contradiction in terms. Cooperate means "to act or work together with another or others for a *common* purpose." The decrees and edicts of authoritarians reflect strictly their own, not common, purposes. In any common cause, the working together has to be private, personal, voluntary. In a word, let each do whatever he pleases so long as it is peaceful. What, then, do we have in common? Each pursuing his uniqueness!

That would be my ideal of freedom: No man-concocted restraints against the release of creative human energy. More precisely, I refer to the free market, private ownership, limited government philosophy with its moral and spiritual antecedents. To me, this is but an ancient, moral axiom—the Golden Rule—expressed in politico-economic terms. You and I can best help each other by tending to our own knitting, pursuing our own uniqueness, respecting the rights of each to the fruits of his own labor, and freely exchanging when and if mutually advantageous—not an iota of coercion! Does this not clarify what we mean when referring to the freedom philosophy!

We have had in the past few decades a remarkable demonstration of the simple life. Yet, few have taken any note of this miracle of simplification—which brings the wealth of the world to our doorstep; they are blind to the wonders they have been experiencing. This makes all the more extraordinary Lord Tennyson's prophetic vision of more than a century ago:

> For I dipt into the future, far as
>   human eye could see,
> Saw the Vision of the world and all
>   the wonders that would be;
> Saw the heavens fill with commerce,
>   argosies of magic sails,
> Pilots of the purple twilight, dropping
>   down with costly bales.

So let us understand and enjoy the simple life—its exclusively voluntary nature, and the unimaginable wisdom which attends the unfettered release of creative energy. Otherwise, if we remain unaware of its blessings, our blindness threatens its termination and promises instead a descent into the complex life of the primitive. For it is an observed fact that the complexities are alarmingly on the increase.

In every instance, the complexities are composed of coercive intrusions by dictocrats in and out of public office. The excuse, of course, is that the intricacies are now too enormous to operate without dictocratic management; these people actually believe that they possess the capabilities needed to make things function. Really, the intricacies are no more numerous than before; all that has happened is a fantastic and wonderful expansion in specialization—division of labor —that is, each to his own uniqueness. This, in turn, has made all of us interdependent. We have here a flowering of the simple life, the continuation of which requires a moral conduct, namely, an observation and practice of the Golden Rule—the way it should be!

Recall that no one knows how to make an ordinary wooden pencil let alone an automobile or a jet plane. But, then, no one understands a cell, a molecule, an atom. You name it! Yet, the dictocrats do not know that they know not. In their behavior they attempt to go beyond their finite minds, which is to say that they are out of their minds, regardless of how brilliant they may appear. It is this coercive intrusion, this unreasonable force, that threatens man's survival.

The way to strive for the simple life is to gain an awareness that the wisdom implicit in its observation is trillions of times greater than exists in you or me or any other discrete individual. Every discovery, invention, insight, intuitive thought, think-of-that since the dawn of human consciousness—the overall luminosity—flows to your and my benefit if we can avoid its nemesis: the complexities of coercive intrusions.

Why should we lose that highest form of moral and economic life—each to his own uniqueness—which we have had the privilege of sampling! Truly, it is a life whose plot is simple.

6

THE FEAR OF
FAILURE AND SUCCESS

*There is great beauty in going
through life without anxiety or
fear. Half our fears are baseless,
and the other half discreditable.*
—CHRISTIAN NESTELL BOVEE

It is not fear or trepidation that keeps one from jumping
out of an airplane without a parachute; it is, instead, an
understanding of the law of gravitation. Fear—in the sense of
being frightened of death or life—is a deadening emotion.
True, fear of danger may help us avoid a senseless risk, but
it is not fear that guides us aright; rather, the guide is a
knowledge of that which advances or retards any worthy
activity. Yet, fear is widespread and it hampers human progress in many areas, including business.

Business is a profit *and loss* affair, and—as it has been
said—

it is just as necessary to the health of a dynamic economy
that dying industries be allowed to die as that growing industries be allowed to grow.[1]

---

[1]See *Economics In One Lesson* by Henry Hazlitt, p. 72, paperback edition.

There are countless business starts in the U.S.A. annually, and a substantial percentage of these turn out to be failures within two or three years. Suppose these businessmen were not allowed to fail, that government would "bail them out" with money taken coercively from all consumers. Within one's lifetime our country would be burdened with tens of thousands of "businesses" producing goods and/or services consumers would not willingly purchase; meanwhile, tax-burdened consumers would have been deprived of the means to purchase what they really want. I say, *let business failures die,* not only in the interest of consumers—all of us—but as a favor to those who have failed.

On this latter point I speak with experience. Back in 1911 the village blacksmith made a popcorn and hamburger wagon for another youngster and me—$12.00. We tried and failed! I am happy now that we did, for that failure put me on the long, long trail of discovering myself. Following World War I, I started a wholesale produce business in Ann Arbor—on a shoestring. After six years of working a 100-hour week, I failed. Back on that long, long trail again. I do not advocate failure as a deliberate business policy. But I am convinced that we may learn from those failures how better to use our faculties and resources.

Serving consumers is a risky business, for they couldn't care less whether any one business venture succeeds or fails. A business begins with what appears to be an opportunity to serve, a hope that consumers will want the product or service enough to return costs plus a profit. But the result may be a failure. Starting a business is a calculated risk, taken in faith rather than in fear. Fear merely retards the chances taken, including the chances of success.

Chances of success? I repeat, it is not fear that guides us aright; fear retards. And we are now the victims of a widespread, debilitating fear. It is the fear—mounting to a phobia—that the free market, private ownership, limited government way of life cannot be trusted to serve our needs and aspirations. We little understand or appreciate the wonders wrought when men are free to act creatively as they choose, in spite of countless daily demonstrations going on before our very eyes. The consequence of such blindness and fear is that statism—coercive collectivism—reaches into ever more areas of business life.

What! Leave mail delivery or education to the free and unfettered market? Leave the determination of wages, hours of labor, or the pricing of goods and services to the competitive process? Might as well allow free entry in the fields of power and light, airlines, railroads, TV, banking! So runs the thoughtless chorus of those who lack knowledge of the miraculous market; in the absence of a belief in its efficacy, the market is bound to be feared. We are afraid to compete.

Fear retards a dynamic economy in more serious ways as well. Reflect on the numerous exclusive franchises to serve given markets—governmental grants allowing no free entry—such as railroads, airlines, power and light, radio and TV channels, and so on. The government which grants these privileges will, as a matter of course, coercively govern that which it bestows. In a word, the free market is displaced by an enormous bureaucracy: the ICC, FTC, FDA, and countless others. In the place of private initiative is political expediency; competing to serve customers gives way to dictatorial edicts; instead of taking entrepreneurial risks, we place our bets on bureaucratic management and control.

When exclusive franchises are bestowed—the purpose being to deny free entry—consumers become dependent on these government-backed monopolies. The fear that these giants might fail is enormous. No power and light, no railroads, no airlines is a frightening prospect. *They must not be allowed to die!* How cope with this danger? Let these privately financed businesses give way to government ownership!

Have a look at the railroad situation. Government control (control is really ownership) has increased year by year. Ability to compete? Why, if a railroad wishes to cut a rate to meet some other form of transport, it takes two or three years of bureaucratic red tape to get approval. Too late! The railroads are failing, and unless there is a reversal of policy, the railroads in America will soon be fully nationalized, as in other countries. And, as in other countries, all citizens, railroad customers or not, will be heavily taxed to defray the fantastic deficits, an inevitable result of government managed businesses.

As this is penned, one of the world's largest power and light companies is petitioning government to bail it out of financial difficulties by purchasing two of its plants—$500 million worth! Project this trend: eventually all power and light nationalized as in other countries!

A major airline is suffering large losses. What to do? Appeal to the Federal government for a subsidy that will compensate for losses! The end result must be an Air America, government owned and operated as is Aeroflot, Air France, Air India, BEA, and so on.

Is it not easy to see how wrong policy—no free entry and thus no competition—leads ever closer to the total state, as in Russia? Wrong policy, once approved and established, induces a near-overwhelming fear and that fear leads to out-and out communism: the state ownership and control of the means of production.

No risk in the societal realm is more senseless than to stake one's life on the authoritarian state. Yet, few seem to shudder at such a prospect. Most citizens show no fear as they gradually plod toward enslavement—no disgust once enslaved. To them, the what-is and the what-ought-to-be are one and the same. Most Russian citizens are as content with their unrecognized plight as most Americans are with ours—and for the same reason: failure to see that there is an alternative.

The alternative? It is this: the free market featured by free entry, open competition, and prices fluctuating in response to supply and demand. In other words, a situation in which any failing business, small or large, is allowed to die, and any successful business, regardless of size, is allowed to grow. Flexibility—the capacity quickly to cope with ever-changing economic circumstances! Not a single dictocratic formula—by governments, labor unions, or whatever—standing against the release of creative human energy. Millions of sources of initiative and creativity replacing know-it-all edicts! Complete freedom in all honest transactions! This is the alternative to all-out statism; there is no other.

Talk about fear! Most people, in and out of government, are scared to death of this alternative. What they fear is the unknown; they are scared of what they imagine things would be like. They see hobgoblins in the form of large, successful businesses that grow ever bigger. In their dread, they imagine one business making all automobiles or all airplanes or producing all power and light. They fantasize such monopolies as being in complete command of the market. What could be worse than this chimera? They fear that one supplier might capture the entire market—and they fear that the government wouldn't take over such a monopolistic structure.

The facts? So long as there is free entry, any successful business, even if it has a particular market all to itself, must serve consumers efficiently if it is to survive. Any such enterprise must operate as if a superior competitor lies in wait. For that would surely be the case at the least lapse of performance and efficiency.

Monopoly? It need not be feared unless backed by coercion. Name an instance! For example, in the 1920's it was a common notion that the Ford Motor Company was so powerful that no other could ever challenge its position. Since the turn of the century there have been about one thousand starts in the auto industry. The failures were allowed to die; the successful ones were allowed to grow. Is there a land of people in all the world better served with autos than Americans?

So let us free ourselves of these unreasonable fears. It is only knowledge that guides us aright. In the politico-economic realm, it is a knowledge of how the free market works its wonders to the benefit of all. We need not fear to put our trust in the market.

7

CONTROLS TELL LIES!

*O, what a goodly outside falsehood
hath, a goodly apple rotten at the
core.*

—SHAKESPEARE

This is not to question self-control or such governmental control as the codification and restraint of destructive actions;
these controls are all to the good. The kind I wish to expose
are the dictocratic controls over the creative actions; these
tell lies—boldfaced and flagrant lies!

My claim: A controlled payment for a wage exacted by
labor unions or government, or a controlled rate for rent,
interest, or goods and services of any kind, *is not a price;* it
is a dictatorial fiction—an economic falsehood. Thus, such a
term as "price control" is a contradiction in terms; it makes
no more sense than "freedom of the press control."

Support for this claim requires no more than casual probing. What is price? The dictionary defines price in this context as "value, worth," and I shall abide by this definition.
Now, suppose I coerce you into paying me $100 per hour for
my services or coercively forbid anyone to pay more than five

cents for your hamburgers. Is it not plain that these figures
have nothing whatsoever to do with the value or worth of my
services or your hamburgers? That they are not prices but
fictions? That they are lies when represented as prices? How
can $100 per hour be said to be the "price" of one's services
or five cents the "price" of a hamburger when no voluntary
exchanges take place at those rates?

Value—price—can be determined in one way and one way
only: by the free and unfettered market. In other words, value
results from a subjective determination based on individual
preferences. Reduced to the simplest terms, a price is what
you or others will freely and willingly exchange for my services or the amount that others will freely and willingly exchange for your hamburgers. Whatever that turns out to be
is value, worth. This figure represents whatever other people
deem our offerings are worth to them. If we willingly swap
your hamburger for my quarter, in this instance, the price of
the hamburger is a quarter and the price of the quarter is a
hamburger. I value the hamburger more than the quarter and
you value the quarter more than the hamburger. Both of us
gain in our respective judgments or there would have been no
exchange, that is, assuming a free and unfettered market.

The monetary figure, whatever the amount, when determined in the above manner, *is price*—all misuse of words to
the contrary notwithstanding.

How can the political fiction of "price control," now on the
rampage, be exposed or seen through? Simple! First, merely
recognize that price is value in terms of money and, second,
reflect on the limitless, ever-changing, personal estimations
of value by you and everyone else. Thus, price must fluctuate
in accord with the ever-changing value judgments it repre-

sents. Price is wedded to value; the two are inseparable for price monetarily mirrors value.

Let us reflect on the fantastic, day-to-day, up-and-down, every-which-way variations in value judgments and then we can see what can be expected by way of price fluctuations— honest representations of changing values. For instance, what value would the Metropolitan Opera in its heyday have put on my services as a singer? Zero value and zero price! On Robert Merrill's service? Very high value and very high price!

The value and price of a hamburger? Were I starving on a life raft, a hamburger would be valued as I value my life, and my offering price the whole of my possessions. Not so, had I just overstuffed at a banquet; a hamburger than would be worthless to me.

What you and I value today may well be valueless to us tomorrow. Auto No. 1 has a high value for which we will pay a high price. Auto No. 10 would have a lesser value to most of us and the price we would offer would be correspondingly less.

So-called price control divorces value and price. The dictocratic monetary figure is unrelated to value, worth. It is a falsehood, as absurd as it can be. What should we call this fiction? It has only one correct name: *people control!*

8

SHORTAGES ARE
HUMAN BLUNDERS

Another mistake, not to call it blunder.

—DANIEL DEFOE

This thesis has nothing to do with such natural shortages as rain on the Sahara, arable soil in the Arctic, or salmon in Great Salt Lake; the characteristic features of Nature are here omitted. These comments have to do solely with what I and many others refer to as shortages in the politico-economic realm—the results of human action.

My dictionary defines shortage as "a deficiency in the quantity or amount *needed*." (Italics mine) This definition might have been written before the discovery of the subjective theory of value in 1870; but more likely the author is some contemporary who fails to grasp this simple economic truth: *The value of any good or service is whatever others will offer in willing exchange.*

True, economics is the study of how to overcome scarcity; there is never enough of everything for everybody. Yet, not enough of this or that for all persons is rarely referred to as a shortage; at least, in my opinion, it should not be. I want to explain why this term should be reserved for the consequences of human blunders. But first we must try to understand *need* as it relates to economic reality.

The goods or services *needed* relate to where and what and when and why and how and who we are. My father, for instance, felt no more need for a TV than did Socrates. Galileo felt no more need for an airplane than Confucius felt the need for a telescope, first developed by Galileo nineteen centuries later. I feel no more need for a good or service that does not yet exist—beyond my ken—than do you.

Needs are responses to feelings or hankerings which, in turn, are set in motion by experiences and situations which vary from one extreme to the other. A millionaire alcoholic in desperation would doubtless pay a thousand dollars for one bottle of booze. That's how high he might value his need. Didn't someone pay $250,000 for one of Hitler's cars? How much would I pay for it? I wouldn't take it as a gift! Imagine the value that some individuals with a collector's bent would put on a Dead Sea scroll—millions of dollars. Why all of this? It is a feeling of need which ranges all the way from casual preferences to passionate cravings. Need and value are economic twins—they correlate in the mind of the individual.

Now observe this fact: We never use the term "shortage" to explain the scarcity of Hitler's cars or of the Dead Sea scrolls, and rarely of any other good or service beyond our means. Should we desire something beyond our reach, we simply say to ourselves, "That price is too high."

To the extent that the market is free, to that extent are we guided by our feeling or need relative to price. Is this not as it should be? This leaves each individual free to exercise his preferences, that is, to satisfy his needs or subjective judgments. If someone prefers to live in an attic rather than in a comfortable home in order that he may acquire rare books, I say, let him live that way. Anything that's peaceful! However, in the practice of this tolerant way of life—the freedom philosophy—be it noted that we rarely apply the term "shortage" to either comfortable homes or rare books. If we do, we shouldn't!

The free and unfettered market is a computer. Fed into it daily are literally trillions of facts from all over the world: a drought here, a blight or hurricane there, fantastic shifts in tastes, value judgments, likes and dislikes, on and on. What answer does the computer give? A price! If the price be attractively high to producers they will turn their talents in that direction; if low, they will concentrate on something else. Thus, the free market is always moving toward an equilibrium of supply and demand. One cannot name a good or service left to the free market—void of coercive interferences —that is referred to as either shortage or surplus.

Of course the market as it presently exists is far from free. False data—human blunders—are fed into it resulting in false prices and erroneous signals to producers and consumers which, in turn, account for all shortages and surpluses. The computer experts have a term for this blundering: GIGO— Garbage In, Garbage Out.[1]

Let me now demonstrate how human blunders bring about a shortage. Make a reasonable assumption: there are ten

---

[1]See "The Greatest Computer on Earth" in my *Anything That's Peaceful* (Irvington-on-Hudson, N.Y.: The Foundation for Economic Education, Inc., 1964) pp. 157-170.

million women who would if they could possess a one-carat diamond ring. The price today is $2,500. The ladies do not think of such rings as being in short supply for they are seen on display in many jewelry stores throughout the country. Would-be consumers only feel they cannot afford such a luxury. Now, assume that I am government's price control czar. Blunder number one! Next, assume that I set a ceiling price on one-carat diamond rings at $50. Blunder number two! Immediately, following these two blunders, there will be a tremendous shortage of such rings. Why? Because there are millions of women who want such a ring and who have $50. Shortages in the economic realm have their origin in such human blunders!

Surpluses are also the result of similar human blunders. The only difference is a ceiling over prices rather than a floor under them. In the latter—wheat, for example—growers produce more as consumers buy less. What to do? How cover up this blunder? Give it to the Russians!

As in the case of the diamond rings, a ceiling over the price of gasoline results in producers letting up and consumers lining up. Such blunders explain the "energy crisis"!

Finally, how are we to account for these blunders? How come the czars and their attempts at economic legerdemain? The answer: the millions of citizens who blunder by either condoning or supporting coercive intrusions into the market. The blunders from which we suffer originate with a blundering citizenry, the millions who fail to grasp the simplest and most important economic fact: the value of any good or service is whatever others will offer in willing exchange.

They do not even try to see that the control we think to exercise over prices actually regulates human action; it is the forcible closure of the market place to producers or to consumers, or to both, thus denying peaceful persons the opportunity to specialize and to trade.

And reflect on the naivete of believing that there is a person, now or ever, who has the competency to manipulate to our advantage the literally trillions of variations in human needs. Why, there is not a single mortal being who knows how to run his own life perfectly, let alone yours or mine. And a nation's population? So absurd it staggers even moderate common sense.

The cure? Mind one's own business. Let everyone else mind his own. Stop seeking or granting special privilege or protection or subsidy or power over other peaceful persons. A fair field, and no favors. Compete openly and freely. Behave responsibly. Give freedom a chance to work its miracles.

9

POLITICAL HOCUS-POCUS

You can fool some of the people all of the time, and all of the people some of the time, but you cannot fool all of the people all of the time.

—LINCOLN

Even those who are not fooled by the political trickery of our time nonetheless find themselves victims of it.

It is not enough to see through this legerdemain; each seer bears a responsibility to help others understand what is wrong, why it is false. Of course, the reason for the current deception-on-the-rampage is that those who are fooled most of the time like it that way. They prefer to believe that "the great white father" will relieve them from thinking and self-responsibility. This nonsense reminds me of the character in the motion picture, *Caesar and Cleopatra,* who knelt at the feet of Caesar exclaiming, "Oh, Caesar, I never knew freedom until I became your slave." Nearer the truth would have been this: "Oh, Caesar, I shall never live in a free country until I find a way to expose your hocus-pocus." Finding that way is my problem.

When authoritarianism in its numerous forms was thought to be appropriate, that is, before the free society was discovered as the enlightened way of life, deception was widely approved as a moral device. The Divine right of kings is an example as is Plato's philosopher-king idea or Machiavelli's advice to the Prince on craftiness and duplicity. And Ratner, Spinoza's biographer, had this to say about one of the great philosophers of all time:

> Far from it being necessary to tell the masses only the truth, Spinoza believed, as did Plato before him, that it may even be necessary in order to rule the masses successfully in the ways of wisdom and virtue to deceive them to a greater or lesser extent. Such deception is, as a political expediency, morally justified, for the rulers would be lying in the interests of virtue and truth.

"Lying in the interest of truth"—a spoof if I ever heard one—should have been phrased, "Lying in the interest of a ruler's egotistical assumption that he knows the truth" and, thus, is qualified to run our lives. If this assumption can be clearly debunked, the political hocus-pocus in the U.S.A. today would be stripped of its pretensions—stark naked for all to behold.

As a starter, assume that I am wiser than any ruler, any dictocrat, ever thought himself to be—a thousand times wiser than I know myself to be. Next, assume that you and I are intimately acquainted—buddies, shall we say. How competent, under such circumstances, would you think I am to rule your life—to dictate what you should think, believe, make, buy, sell, what your aspirations should be; in a word, how you should live this earthly life? Should you accept me as such a god, then you are one who, as Lincoln proclaimed, can be fooled all the time. My condolences!

Assuming that you are aware of my inability to run your life beneficially—regardless of our intimacy and my wisdom— let us have a look at our nation's political rulers. The number grows apace! Those elected or appointed to governmental offices—federal, state, and local, excluding the military—must, by now, total approximately 16,000,000.[1] Bear in mind, further, that governments today are given more to controlling the citizenry than to protecting life and livelihood.

Why this departure from America's original design of protecting life and livelihood, invoking a common justice—keeping the peace? No one knows all the reasons. But one is obvious: intimacy has all but disappeared. Why, I do not even know the Mayor of my village, nor does he know me. The same lack of intimacy applies to the countless thousands in New York State, and to the 3,000,000 politicians and bureaucrats in the Federal establishment.

Why so much emphasis on intimacy? Just this: the less those vested with coercive powers know of our existence, the more they coercively manage our lives. Hardly a one of them would exert such hocus-pocus on a man-to-man basis. Face-to-face such folly would be apparent even to Caesar. *It is when we become unknowns that they "know" how to run our lives.* This thought, seriously considered, begins to reveal the chicanery that plagues us.

Does this chicanery reach its apogee at the Federal level?

[1]According to the 1973 *Statistical Abstract of the United States,* citing 1972 figures, the total was 13,500,000. The growth has been substantial during the past two years.

It would seem so when we reflect on the origin of wage, price, production, and exchange controls; the manipulation of *our* money; what portion of *our* own labor is ours; medicare and social security—controls by the thousands! Yet, at the state and local levels we observe government education, zoning and land use, garbage disposal, recreation pools and parks, licensing of businesses and professions, government busing— you name it! In principle, there is no difference between the coercion which stems from my village and that which arises in the national capital.

What all of this boils down to is that these politicians and bureaucrats—Federal, state, and local—have no more competence to run your life or mine than I have to run yours. The power they exercise affords them no better idea of our millions of diverse needs, aspirations, ideas, ideals, talents, abilities than was known by cavemen eons ago. To these rulers— and it cannot be otherwise once this false role is assumed— you are nothing more than a manipulable statistic. And, in their eyes, that's all you are—just a number!

If you and I are just numbers, then what shall we say of the Mayors, Governors, the President of the United States, or any one of the 16,000,000 in the more than 100,000 governments in our country? Yet, those who brazenly treat other human beings as numbers seldom so berate themselves. Why this aberration? As Lord Acton phrased it, "Power tends to corrupt, and absolute power corrupts absolutely."

The mere thought that I can run your life better than you can is corrupting. By so thinking, I set myself apart, that is, I assume the role of a god and relegate you to the status of a number—the big I-Am, the nonhuman you. Again, a spoof!

Doubtless there are many ways by which to expose this

political hocus-pocus. All of us should have a fling at it. The late Sumner H. Slichter, Harvard economist, brought the exposure into focus May 17, 1947:

> Our economy has the tremendous advantage of possessing three and a half million business enterprises outside of agriculture and about six million business enterprises in agriculture. This means that the American economy has nearly ten million places where innovations may be authorized. Have you ever thought of that? Ten million places where experiments may be tried, where no further authority is needed to authorize an experiment. Our economy operates under about ten million separate private business budgets. No regimented economy can hope to compete in dynamic drive with an economy which possesses nearly ten million independent centers of initiative.

Slichter's point, enlightening as it is, only points in the right direction. The real exposure, at least as it occurs to me, is stronger by many, many times.

You Are Extraordinary is the title the eminent biochemist, Dr. Roger Williams, gave one of his books. The "you" to whom he refers is each of us, in or out of public office. Why is each individual extraordinary? No two persons are alike as to talents, abilities, ambitions, needs, aspirations, or in any other way. Dissimilarity—variation—may well be the only characteristic all of us have in common.

Let us begin with the 16,000,000 public officials. Write the name of each on separate pieces of paper; toss them into a stiff wind, and pick out one at random. It turns out to be Joe Doakes. Joe, if carefully scrutinized, will be found to have several unique talents of one sort or another. He may excel at mental arithmetic, as an engineer, a piccolo player, golfer, rhymer of words, grower of posies, cook, cabinet maker, or whatever. No other person on earth possesses talents identical to his. Next, it is safe to guess that each of these public officials is unique in at least ten ways. So, to get an idea of just how many creative and unique talents exist among this part of the population—the "ins"—simply multiply 16,000,000 times 10: 160,000,000!

Be it noted that I am conceding a fantastic creativity to our public officials—and for good reasons. First, this is a truth, though little recognized. Second, hardly a one of them will reject this accolade. Agreement! Third, once this point is accepted by them, they ought to see the logic of making a similar concession to the more than 100,000,000 adults not in public office. Multiply the "outs"—the you's and me's—by 10 and the answer is one billion unique, creative talents.

Now to my point: Joe Doakes, be he Mayor, Governor, President, or whoever, limited as he is in his own perceptions —no more omniscient than are the rest of us—is utterly incapable of controlling beneficially 1,000,000,000 creative talents. Why? Because he has relatively few talents of his own. My attempting to dictate what a Thomas Alva Edison should invent would be far less absurd.

Were I to accept such power over an Edison—or over you— that very acceptance would corrupt me to the point of dictatorial behavior. I would lose all sight of my limitations, my lack of competence or judgment on many matters; I would become a party to the hocus-pocus which so disastrously plagues the U.S.A. today.

Little man, the creative potential of the universe flows through you. It is within your power to either clog the conduits or increase your capacity. Growth and enlargement of self is the aim, for we have been given creativity as a goal, a talent to bolster and to bring to bloom, not to thwart Partake in the political apparatus only to restrain and inhibit interferences with creativity. Encourage this God-given potentiality to flower as far as is humanly possible in each and every one of us.

10

WIZARDRY

The wily wizard must be caught.
—DRYDEN

Who is the "wily wizard" that must be caught? His name is legion, and millions are under his charm. He is, as the dictionary puts it, "clever . . . but understood as wise." It's not only the millions who mistake the wizard's cleverness for wisdom; he believes himself to be wise! Who is he? Unfortunately, there are countless thousands of these wily wizards—charming us into socialism.

First, let us clearly identify this socialism or communism or fascism—call authoritarianism what you will:

Socialism is the state ownership or control of the *means* of production (the planned economy) and/or the state ownership or control of the *results* of production (the welfare state).

Bear in mind that ownership and control amount to the same thing. One really owns whatever he controls, and he controls what he owns. The things a person does not control are not his own!

So, who are the wizards? Who dreams up and imposes wage, price, production, and exchange controls, sets the hours and terms of labor, introduces social security, medicare, food stamps, and countless other phases of the planned economy and the welfare state?

At this point let me challenge a widely held notion. Our plunge into socialism is *not* because of a conspiracy on the part of Russian communists! Those folks on the other side of the Iron Curtain have very little to do with our plight. The real motivators of socialism in America are the wily wizards in our own population. The first question is: How can they be identified? And, next, how can they be caught? These are the questions I shall attempt to answer.

What is the characteristic that earmarks an individual as a wily wizard? It is mankind's most destructive affliction: the little-god syndrome, the utterly nonsensical notion that some philosopher king could, if given the coercive power to do so, run your life and mine better than we can. Unaware of how low he is on the scale of infinite intelligence, he would dictate even our aspirations. He would direct what we think, drink, eat, where we should work and for how much, what and with whom we must exchange, the purposes for which the fruits of our labor are to be spent, what we may or may not buy; in a word, we are to be carbon copies or duplicates of a self-styled god. He and his tribe are the real authors of socialism in America!

It is easily demonstrable that no single person on earth knows how to make a simple wooden lead pencil. How preposterous for any person to believe he can make another individual in his image, let alone 220 million human beings!

Those who have not reflected on this matter are likely to think that no such wily wizards exist, that my contentions are far-fetched. Well, they are not. The wily wizards range from so-called economists and political scientists to political office-holders. They are to be found among educators, clergy, labor officials, and businessmen. And, unless we have stayed away from the polls, the chances are that all of us have voted for many office seekers who are afflicted with wizardry, more or less.

Example: We do not know what is good for us, but the wizard does. For instance, should we drive our old car rather than buy a new one? How does the wizard propose to decide for us? Place a heavy tax on new cars, thus reducing the demand, the enlarged tax making it possible for the government to do more and more things for us that we are unable to do for ourselves. Freedom of choice would be denied to everyone except the wizard.

Is this a conjured-up example? No, it is real, just one of thousands of schemes to run our lives. While all are of the same coercive pattern, no two are any more identical than are the ideas and preferences of any of the rest of us. This example, however, serves to expose the fallacy of all such coercive schemes.

Let us assume that all of the wily wizards had had their varying dictatorial ways, say since 1865. There would be no telephones or power and light or dishwashers or tissue papers or airplanes or thousands of other conveniences. Indeed, there would be no automobiles for them to regulate or control or tax. Why this claim?

Coercion is not a creative force. No idea, discovery, invention, insight, intuitive flash ever issued from an edict, however well-intended. Creativity is exclusively the out-pouring of human energy not in bondage, of men when free to think, to dream, to imagine, to explore the limitless not-yet. Coercion can only inhibit and penalize—nothing more! Testimony? The American experience which witnessed the greatest outburst of creative energy in all history. Why? Human freedom in greater measure than ever before!

What would the wily wizard think were I to turn the tables, that is, accept his "reasoning" and impose it on him?

To repeat, he insists that our priorities are distorted and that, among other things, we should drive old rather than new automobiles, that he knows better than we what our goals and priorities should be. He does not like our penchant for new cars. To achieve his aim, he would tax new cars off the market. Further, the increased revenue would permit government to do for us what we are "unable" to do for ourselves.

Very well! Suppose I do not favor the wily wizard. To get my way, I shall use his method: tax his livelihood to the point of starvation. Life is impossible without livelihood. I would be rid of him as he would be rid of new cars. I'll wager he wouldn't buy his own wizardry when turned on him any more than I buy his when turned on me. What would I have government do with the increased revenue? Let it do for him that which he, starved to death, would be unable to do for himself! What could government do to better his plight in his situation? No more than it can do for me in my situation!

I agree with Dryden—the wily wizard must be caught. But how? Would I really try to get rid of him as he would rid us of new cars? Of course not; no freedom devotee would ever

Don't fight coercion
with more coercion!

resort to any such primitive means of attaining his ends. As
Ortega phrases it, "Lucifer is the patron saint of mere neg-
ativistic revolt . . . even though we freely admit that most of
the things revolted against deserve to be buried away."

How then should we go about resolving our conflicting and
varying value judgments, admittedly at sixes and sevens? No
two of us have precisely the same ideas of what ought and
ought not to be; indeed, yours and mine are in constant flux;
no one except a mummy ever stays put. My answer: dialogue,
free and open discussion, you airing your thoughts, I mine.
This is the way to emerge in awareness, to gain enlightenment, to discover truth—now and than a glimmer from you, or
perhaps from me. *It is this freedom in discourse that assures
ascendancy!*

There are two appropriate ways open to freedom devotees
—ways that go hand-in-hand. The first is to think through and
explain with all the clarity one can command the fallacy of
every totalitarian notion that rears its ugly head, those notions put forth by the wily wizards. I have yet to hear or read
one of these notions that cannot be laid bare. Does this mean
that you and I must go it alone? No, we can and should help
each other in this respect.[4]

The second way presents the real challenge, namely,
making the case for the free market, private ownership, limited government way of life, along with its moral and spiritual antecedents, far and away better than anyone has yet
done. My confession and contention: No one of us, here or
elsewhere, past or present, has more than scratched the surface in making the case for freedom. To set the stage for my

---

[4]See *Cliches of Socialism,* 76 attempts to be of help to others. The Foundation for Economic Education, Inc., Irvington-on-Hudson, New York.

concluding point, here are a few thoughts by the eminent French philosopher, Alexis de Tocqueville:

> The soil is productive less by reason of its natural fertility than because the people tilling it are free. . . . Some nations have freedom in the blood. . . . Other nations, once they have grown prosperous, lose interest in freedom and let it be snatched from them without lifting a hand to defend it, lest they should endanger thus the comforts that, in fact, they owe to it alone. It is easy to see that what is lacking in such nations is a genuine love of freedom, that lofty aspiration which (I confess) defies analysis. For it is something one must *feel* and logic has no part in it.[5]

Why did Tocqueville confess that freedom is sustained only by a feeling or love, and that logic has no part in it? Simply this: He, as others of us, failed to make a breakthrough. The generally unrecognized fact? Freedom can be supported by logic just as authoritarianism can be dethroned by logic. Nor will freedom ever reign for long in the absence of logical exposition. Mere feelings are fickle products of the emotions, and have no stability. Feelings are subject no less to inanities heard on every hand than to rare wisdom. Feelings come and go with the winds that blow.

The challenge? It is for a few—assured if many try—to achieve a logical explanation of freedom and its wondrous powers for what is good, right, creative—difficult and seemingly impossible as it is. As I see it, such an attainment is a necessary step in the Cosmic Plan; it is our privileged role in the evolution of man, in the emergence of self. The more we emerge or evolve, the greater will be the intellectual de-

---

[5]See *The Old Regime and the French Revolution* by Alexis de Tocqueville, (Garden City, N.Y.: Doubleday & Company, Inc., 1955) p. 169.

mands upon us. This is as it should be. And look upon this challenge not as a troublesome chore but rather as a blessed opportunity, a phase of creation.

To cite Ortega again: "The only true revolt is creation— the revolt against nothingness." By revolting against nothingness we attain creativity and the wily wizards are caught; their ways become naught!

11

REFLECTIONS ON
GULLIBILITY

Quick sensitiveness is inseparable
from a ready understanding.
—ADDISON

We live in an age when superstition flourishes and quackery
abounds. This is a credulous generation eager to swallow any
political nostrum—the more absurd the better. I fully concur
with this opinion by Professor W. A. Paton:

> As an adjective to describe present-day attitudes, aims, and
> popular proposals for dealing with current economic prob-
> lems, real or pseudo, the term "gullible" is a much more
> appropriate label for our society than "good" or "great."[1]

Very few, indeed, are those among us who have any awareness of the current gullibility—a blindness pervades the population. Short of a more general realization of this intellectual
insensitivity, our society is doomed; it must fall into a sham-

---

[1]See "The Gullible Society," *The Freeman,* March, 1974.

bles. Sensing this formidable situation, as does Professor Paton, is assuredly the first step in gaining any relief. However, two more steps would seem to be necessary: (1) discovering the cause of gullibility and (2) finding its remedy, if there be one.

In my view, insensitiveness is the cause of gullibility. A recent experience: Ahead of me in the check-out line at the supermarket was a women with many items in her basket. She paid with government food stamps, totally insensitive to the fact that I would be interested, as one who was financing her purchases. Utterly numb as to gratitude! And most taxpayers, in my place, would have been equally insensitive to their role in paying for that food.

I do not know what the total bill might have been for the food the woman had in her basket. Nor do I know precisely the value of the food stamps she receives each year. But I did find, upon doing a bit of research, that the total U.S. food stamp program that cost $85.5 million in 1965 is projected to cost $7.2 billion in 1975. Was I gullible, were all of us gullible, in allowing the small beginnings of a program that would expand by 8,400 per cent in ten years!

And how many Americans are expected to be riding that $7.2 billion gravy train in 1975? The number, I am informed, will be 16,000,000. So if the woman in the supermarket is typical, she will be carrying $450 worth of groceries past the check-out counter, for stamps, in 1975.

In double-checking my estimate of taxes to be paid in 1975 —and calculating the impact on me for a $7.2 billion expenditure—I find that, in effect, I will be paying for about half of that woman's food-stamp purchases. And I do not know her! Should I or should I not be giving some strange woman $225 worth of groceries a year? Do I know if her need is greater than that of any other customer? Or am I simply being gullible about food stamps and many other welfare programs, programs to which I am insensitive, since I do not know the real need for such handouts or know the effect of those handouts on either the recipients or the other taxpayers who will help foot the bill?

How account for this two-sided gullibility—exhibited equally by those who feed at the public trough and those who are forced to keep it filled? Doubtless there are unfathomable reasons—faults and shortcomings interacting on each other—too complex for clear-cut analysis. Were there a single cause, we might readily overcome this insensitiveness—alertness then would be a possibility. However, if a few likely causes can be identified, they may help us see our gullibility and bring some helpful responses from me, you, and some others; any switch would have to be an individual attainment.

The Roman, Horace, some twenty centuries ago, offers one reason which can hardly be questioned:

Adversity has the effect of eliciting talents which in prosperous circumstances would have lain dormant.

Prosperous circumstances! Never in the world's history have any people remotely approached the prosperity we Americans have experienced, and we are generally flabby in consequence. *Gullibility is nothing more nor less than talents lying dormant.* This appears to be an accurate diagnosis of our condition.

Free market, private ownership, limited government practices have been more nearly approximated in the U.S.A. than elsewhere. As a consequence, there has been the greatest release of creative energy ever known: goods and services have flowed in unprecedented abundance to the masses as if manna from Heaven.

Merely reflect upon the material things—tens of thousands —which are available in exchange for doing relatively little, if anything.[2] Note the countless persons who enjoy a fantastic affluence and do nothing at all. When people get it into their heads that their prosperity is a natural phenomenon as a sunrise, for instance, requiring no talents on their part, talents fail to evolve; in a word, they lie dormant. These people see nothing simply because they are unaware that there is anything to see.

Another likely cause: an astonishing loss of faith in Judeo-Christian charity. Indeed, few in today's world are aware of what it is, let alone the wonders wrought by its practice. That woman at the check-out line had no more gratitude for her something-for-nothing food than the average taxpayer has gratitude for the privilege of filling the trough. Grover Cleveland, in vetoing a handout to drought-stricken Texans, wrote:

> The friendliness and charity of our countrymen can always be relied upon to relieve their fellow-citizens in misfortune. . . . Federal aid in such cases encourages the expectation of paternal care on the part of the Government and weakens the sturdiness of our national character, *while it prevents the indulgence among our people of that kindly sentiment and conduct which strengthens the bonds of a common brotherhood.*

The Congressmen who approved that appropriation doubt-

---

[2]See "Confessions of a Rich Man" in my *Let Freedom Reign* (Irvington-on-Hudson, N.Y.: The Foundation for Economic Education, Inc., 1969) pp. 50-56.

less did so with the best of intentions. They, as distinguished from President Cleveland, were insensitive to charity as a character-building means to deal with misfortune; they could think only of government handouts. This calls to mind a verse packed full of wisdom:

> Oh, were evil always ugly;
> What a boon to virtue that would be!
> But oft it wears a pretty face,
> And lets us cheat unknowingly.

It is an observed fact that whenever government pre-empts any activity, that is, when coercion takes over, voluntary ways are not only forgotten but faith in their efficacy ceases. How many, for instance, believe that mail could be delivered ever so much more efficiently if left to the free market? Only a person now and then! Similarly with charity. When government moves in, charitable practices tend to wither away. Your neighbor is hungry. Today? That's the government's problem, we say. Suppose the government had not intervened. What would you or I do? We would share our loaf of bread!

Were government handouts looked upon as ugly, charity would thrive. But because they are well-intentioned and thus have a pretty face, we cheat each other unknowingly, insensitively. Result: gullibility!

What possibly can be the cure for this gullibility? What can restore alertness? Assuredly, the answer lies half-hidden or it would be generally known and observed; few would label themselves, or like to be labelled, gullible. An obvious answer to gullibility is thinking for self rather than imitating platitudes, plausibilities, popular cliches. But that is too obvious.

The real question is, what can inspire or encourage one to do his own thinking? What is the overlooked formula?

Here's mine: *Count your blessings!* Until now I have looked upon this as the remedy for perhaps the greatest of all evils: covetousness or envy. I am now convinced that it is also the cure for gullibility.

For this practice to have any meaning, to affect one's intellectual demeanor, it would have to be a daily exercise—in a word, habitual and systematic exploration. At first blush, at least to those who have not reflected on their blessings, this is no more of a challenge than a daily repetition of the alphabet, so few blessings are most people aware of.

What I am suggesting is the discovery of one or more heretofore unknown blessings every day of one's life. There aren't that many? Their number is infinite, a world without end! They include every bit of wisdom since the human race began; they range from soaps to soups to tissues to dishwashers; from raindrops to bathtubs; from pets to friends past and present; from atoms to red blood cells to galaxies; from electricity to sunbeams; from blades of grass to the shade of trees; from hot and cold running water to still lakes and wavy seas; from paintings to all the beauties of earth and the heavens. They include every freedom to be the creative self one possesses. World without end!

The daily exploration of one's blessings opens the mind to Infinite Consciousness. This of itself is thinking for self; it is the downing of gullibility. For today, I count among my blessings the ability to share these thoughts with you, whoever you are.

12

THE BLESSINGS
OF DIVERSITY

Were all alike, instead of free,
T'would mean the end of me and thee.

There is an old wheeze that goes something like this: "The whole world is queer but thee and me, and sometimes I think thee a trifle peculiar." The line affixes a bit of humor to a lamentable fact: most people are addicted to conformity. The truth? Were all like thee or me, all would perish. So, let's make the case for diversity.

The first part of the case is easy. Were everyone alike, would we be all men—or all women? There wouldn't even be an Adam and Eve situation, only an uninhabited Eden! Suppose all of us were identical in food preference to those who eat nothing but fish. The fish supply would diminish to the point that all would starve—or die fishing. A moment's reflection reveals the nonsense of be-like-me-ness as related to the strictly physical aspects of our lives—even were all identical to thee or me.

It is when we move from functions of the body to those of the mind that the case for diversity most needs to be examined. People, by and large, seem instinctively to resist the idea of diversity in thinking. Why do not others think and believe as you or I do? Had a person of my convictions lived in Athens twenty-three centuries ago, his disagreement with Plato's concept of a philosopher-king surely would have disturbed the great thinker, even as you and I tend to be disturbed by those who do not see eye to eye with us.

The philosopher-king idea assumes an overlord—absolute rulership—someone who will direct what millions of citizens shall do and how they shall behave. Thinking for self is precluded; the king will do that for us.

Until recent times, kingship—czar, der Fuhrer, the Mikado, a ruler by whatever label—was generally accepted as the only alternative to societal chaos. There had to be a ruler—despite the miserable record—or society would collapse.

Why the failures? Plato's implication is that power hitherto had not been united to wisdom in one man. Obviously, kingship is not to be trusted to power-crazed shallowpates. Plato's solution? Let only philosophers be kings! Then all of a nation's citizens would be blessed, being the beneficiaries of the king's wisdom.

Now, just who is it that qualifies as a philosopher? How designated? There are two ways. First is self-designation. Though not aspiring to kingship, Plato no doubt thought of himself as a philosopher. Look around at our contemporaries. Observe the countless thousands, none of whom doubts his own wisdom; each in his judgment the perfect philosopher. And fit for kingship!

The second way to be labeled a philosopher is by popular

designation. Reflect on those thus acclaimed, ranging from Confucius, Socrates, Plato, Maimonides, Machiavelli, Marx, Berdyaev, to several of our time. Go over the whole list, read of their ideas, and find one competent to rule our lives. Not one remotely qualifies. No such individual ever existed or ever will. And the genuine philosopher, at least of our time, would shun rule, even if it were offered!

Granted, each of these philosophers was in search of truth. Their findings? No two the same! One came upon an idea here, another there; and then a bit of truth, occasionally an out-and-out error, such as Plato's philosopher-king or Marx's "from each according to ability, to each according to need." The worst that could befall mankind would be to give any one philosopher the power to impose his limited vision on everyone else—including other philosophers. Each of us should strive to live by such wisdom as he can glean, while working to expand his vision. But there is no short cut to the attainment of this objective.

When one first reflects on the blessings of diversity in thinking, he might want to make an exception: should not the devotees of liberty look askance at anti-freedom thinking? Of what possible help are Marx and Engels and the countless other opponents? My answer: They are an absolute necessity to the furtherance of our ideal, to the attainment of our aspirations. Bluntly, there is no way to go uphill except as there be hills to climb. In other words, we have no chance of moving toward or perfecting the freedom way of life short of obstacles to overcome—now and forever! It is in the discernment of error that truth comes to light. The art of becoming is composed of acts of overcoming.

Let us suppose that no one today knows any more about

the freedom philosophy than I knew some forty years ago.
Heaven forbid! What jolted me awake? Not someone agreeing with me; it was the system of wage, price and exchange
controls—the National Industrial Recovery Act. This was not
exactly the philosopher-king, but almost as bad: the politi-
cian-bureaucrat. Knowing that to be wrong, I had to explore,
look for, try to discover what is right. The wrong gave me a
toehold, as we say; it served as a stimulant, a springboard.
But for NIRA or some similar wrong, I might well have
remained ideologically disinterested. So, was not the NIRA
a blessing of diversity?

Nearly everyone can recall similar experiences, his thought
processes stimulated by one or two wrongs. But how easy it
is to believe that a few leaps upward in learning suffice. A
momentary awakening and then falling to sleep again!
Worse than falling asleep, however, is to harbor the illusion of
journey's end, the thought that one's job is done.

During the past four decades, since shocked into awareness by NIRA, I have reacted to every anti-freedom notion
that has come to my attention. This has been my "magnificent obsession." The reward? In all modesty, I am far better
informed about such matters than I was some forty years
ago. Yet, the road looms ahead, and I have much further to
go.

To highlight the danger of stagnation, let it be assumed
that I understand far more than I now do—that I have
become better than anyone else! Arrival? Indeed not; whatever the stage, it is only the beginning. However far one trav-
els from his beginning in ignorance, it is but a start toward
the infinite unknown.

Hold the fantasy for a moment: that I have become better

than all others. Then assume that the thoughts of everyone were identical to mine. A better world? No! Such would spell the end of human evolution or emergence—mankind in a state of stagnation.

To seek Truth is to pursue the Infinite. The more one advances, the further into the distance stretches the road ahead. The more one knows, the more he knows there is to know.

Human freedom is an aspiration, never to be perfectly achieved but, at best, only to be more closely approximated. Have no fear of diverse ideas. Welcome them! They are blessings, perhaps in disguise, but steppingstones, nonetheless.

13

THE COMMONERS

As common as all-get-out.
—WILLIAM HAZLITT

My dictionary defines a commoner as "a person not of the nobility: member of the common people."

This definition derives from medieval ranking. The nobility was composed of those in the titled aristocracy under the King: Dukes, Earls, Lords of the Manor, and the like. Most of the others—the millions not "graced" with special, political privilege—were commoners. In principle, this kind of ranking is not to be distinguished from the caste system. In a word, old hat!

Times have changed, which suggests that it is high time to redefine our terms. Who in today's America are commoners and who are aristocrats? It is important that you and I find out for ourselves where our membership belongs. A commoner or an aristocrat? That's the question!

Why should we not think of a commoner as one whose way of life is most common? If persons are assessed in this sensible manner, then the present situation is reversed from what it was in medieval times. Today's commoners occupy the same status as the aristocrats of yore: people "graced" with special, political privilege.

I shall not include as a commoner all of the individuals who in one way or another feed at the public trough. Every last one of us does, willingly or *unwillingly*. Excluded are the very few who unwillingly do so, whose proclaimed positions are against any special privilege for self or others. Subtract these few and the rest are commoners, the countless millions who favor and plead for one or more of the thousands of governmental handouts and special privileges. So common today is the plundering trait that only now and then can an individual be found who will have none of it. Everyone who declares, "but I must make an exception in this instance," is a commoner. To claim that this class may account for 99 per cent of the adult population borders on an understatement!

Nothing is to be gained by classifying most of the population as commoners unless some light can be shed as to *why* this sad state of affairs. Doubtless there are more reasons than we know or even suspect, but a few are more or less obvious.

While any number of people may demonstrate expertise at this or that—skilled in their chosen fields—most of them, when it comes to politico-economic matters, have no ideas of their own. They are simply borne along by whatever wave of opinion happens to predominate at any given time. Imitators, at best! Who do these masses tend to imitate? Those with great coercive or political power, those with much wealth, and those who are highly celebrated. These are their pied pipers!

If imitation makes commoners of the millions, it would

seem to follow that the imitated themselves are commoners. And, with but few exemplarly exceptions, they are. Why? Let's speculate on the reasons for commonality among the politically powerful, the wealthy, and the celebrated. Why in this order? Power to run the lives of others has a greater attraction than either wealth or fame. Wealth is in second place, and fame trails by a slim margin.

It was Lord Acton who wrote, "Power tends to corrupt and absolute power corrupts absolutely." Our Founding Fathers were well aware of this danger when they drafted the Constitution and the Bill of Rights so they set bounds to political power, more severely limiting its exercise than ever before in history. As a consequence, fewer elected and appointed officials corrupted themselves during these early decades than in any previous period.

Lord Acton's "tends" is an important modifier. The mere possession of power does not necessarily corrupt the individual; it only tends to do so and in most cases does. All of us have the power to interfere in the creative lives of others, but there is no corruption if we refuse to exercise that power. It is only the *use* of coercive power that corrupts the individual.

An example of the tendency overcome: Lorenzo the Magnificent! The Duke of Florence—its ruler with unlimited power—was not corrupted. Why? Instead of using his power to interfere with the creative activity of the Florentians, he gave of his talents and great wealth to assist them in this respect. He was "one of the towering figures of the Italian Renaissance."

An example of the tendency not overcome: Piero, Lorenzo's son, who became the Duke of Florence following his father's death. He *used* his power and was corrupted to the point that the Florentians ran the Medici out of Florence. Good riddance!

What is it about power used to run other people's lives that corrupts the holders thereof? To exercise power thusly requires a belief that such action is right. The belief, when examined, turns out to be the illusion of *self-omnipotence,* the assessment of self as a know-it-all. Thinking of one's self as a god—the illusion—is itself the corruption. It is this disease among the power-drunk elite—commoners themselves—that leads in making commoners out of the tag-along masses.

In a second place among the imitated are the very wealthy. I am acquainted with a few millionaires who look upon their wealth not as an end in itself but as a means to higher goals; it frees them from the drudgery—doing all of life's chores one's self—which poverty imposes. Their wealth permits them to pursue their own unique and higher goals, such as the improvement of self, by exchanging their special goods and/or services with others. In a word, wealth, when viewed aright, is the hallmark of a society where the thousand and one chores of life are accomplished by the division of labor, so that each person has the leisure in which to concentrate on his own uniqueness.

Parenthetically, countless millions of us are wealthy, that is, able to exchange our minuscule offerings for life's necessities. Why are there so many of us? The power of a free as distinguished from a coercive or political market—the voluntary way of life on a scale never before known. Indeed, we are so numerous that we fail to stand out; we are more the rule than the exception. It is the very wealthy, not my kind, who are envied.

We must not forget, however, that the great opportunities

wealth provides also mean risks, as we know from the Gold-smith line, "Where wealth accumulates and men decay." Thus, the ones whom prosperity does not adversely affect are few and far between. Living "high on the hog"—ostentation, display, flaunting "success"—features their behavior. Wealth to them is a means to get out of rather than ever deeper into life: year-around vacations, retirement, leisure in the nonpro-ductive sense.

These commoners among the very wealthy inspire envy—corruption—on the grand scale. "Keeping up with the Joneses" is the mode of our times. How to do it? Run to the govern-ment trough! For pittances? Hardly! There are some farm outfits, for instance—commoners—receiving from the govern-ment—all of us—several millions of dollars annually for not farming!

Last, but not to be ignored, are the celebrated. Fame is heady stuff, intoxicating, to say the least. Most people are elated by renown, deserved or not, big scale or small. An applauding audience puffs them up; mention on TV or pic-tures in the press swell their egos. As the Bible has it, "For they loved the praise of man more than the praise of God." This is to say that they rate flattery higher than the discern-ment of truth. Commoners like these have imitators by the millions!

The few exceptions are those who, when flattered, compare the overesteem with their own acute awareness of how little they know. The disparity between the two, more likely than not, results in depression rather than elation. How short I am from what they think I am!

Now to the aristocrats of our time. They may be no more numerous, relative to population, than the titled aristocrats in medieval days, but they differ from them as much as present day commoners differ from the commoners of yore. An about-face in both cases!

These contemporary aristocrats are not easily identifiable. To set our sights aright, let us seek the guidance of two outstanding American Statesmen. Wrote George Washington:

> If, to please the people, we offer what we ourselves disapprove, how can we afterwards defend our work? *Let us raise a standard to which the wise and honest can repair.* The event is in the hand of God.

There you have it: raising high the standard and living by it is the fundamental achievement of the aristocratic spirit. Thomas Jefferson gave this exemplarity an appropriate definition:

> There is a natural aristocracy among men; it is composed of virtues and talents.

Very well! Look around you and within and find those who are not among the modern commoners, those who can truly be numbered among the aristocrats of our time—the new nobility. What are the earmarks of this new breed? Exemplars are not and cannot be apparent to the casual eye; they have to be searched for and discovered. Here are some characteristics:

- Now and then there is a potentially powerful person who refuses to exercise his power over the creative activities of others.
- Occasionally, one will find a very wealthy person who continues to grow, evolve, emerge, hatch—search for truth. No decay!
- And if one looks hard enough, he may find a few celebrated persons whom fame has not intoxicated.

- By and large, however, the aristocrats are to be found among those not distinguished by power, fortune, or fame—the unsung, the unheard of. He or she may be your neighbor, maid, gardener, or chauffeur; or perhaps a young student who is thinking, an oldster who is coming to himself, or an airline pilot who is as much committed to righteousness as to his airport destination.

Two final thoughts: First, the new aristocrats do not think of themselves as such and, thus, wear no labels. And, second, no one will be able to make a single discovery of these uncommon individuals if he be a commoner himself, for as the philosophers say "knowing is the mode of being," or what you are limits what you may know. Therefore, one is ill-advised to even look unless he is struggling to be an exemplar of virtues and talents—a standard setter! Be a seeker, confident that the search is not in vain.

14

LAW VERSUS TYRANNY

*Morality once shattered destroys
the people and the ruler. Outside
of prison and this side of hell men
are not bound together by the club
but by the consciousness of moral
obligations.*

—WALTER A. LUNDEN

According to Thomas Fuller, the 18th century Royalist historian and preacher: "Law governs man; reason the law."
This doesn't seem right to me or, at least, seems contradictory to Professor Lunden's observation about moral obligations.

Does reason govern law? If so, reason would appear to be a low-grade faculty, for there are as many varying conceptions of "law" as there are persons who use the term. Indeed, most of us use "law" loosely, meaning now this and then that. Were reason to govern, it would seem, at the very least, that we should have a sounder conception of what law is than is now the case.

In this context, what is law? Is it a body of legal edicts backed by force? Or a consciousness of moral obligations? Or, if some combination of the two, which takes precedence? These and many other related questions need some careful reflection if reason is to govern.

Lord Keynes, in 1938, speaking of the time when he was twenty, said of himself and his friends:

> We repudiated entirely customary morals, conventions, and traditional wisdom. We were . . . in the strict sense of the term, immoralists . . . we recognized no moral obligation, no inner sanction, to conform or obey. Before heaven we claimed to be our own judge in our own case. So far as I am concerned, it is too late to change; I remain and always will remain, an immoralist. . . .

In a recent comment on that passage, Henry Hazlitt suggests that "it is the spread of precisely this attitude since then to ever-widening circles that helps to explain the moral and political decay in the last few decades."

In answer to the question, Which takes precedence, a body of legal edicts backed by force—the club—or a consciousness of moral obligations?, I say, contrary to Keynes, the latter. In describing himself as an immoralist, Lord Keynes was saying that no moral laws or ethical imperatives are to stand in the way of desires and actions or to otherwise restrict his thoughts and deeds. And the result is an outpouring of legal edicts inspired by him and his disciples and designed to control the affairs of society.

Now to my faith. I proudly profess to being a moralist or an ethicist. I subscribe to the proposition that there are laws of nature and the universe, of Creation, that should be discovered and respected. I believe that all man-made laws—

legal edicts—which go beyond codifying and complementing the moral law serve not to bind men together but to spread them asunder, creating chaos rather than harmony, tyranny rather than peaceful order.[1]

Fundamental to my faith is the rejection of government as the *sovereign* power. This puts me on the side of the writers of the Declaration of Independence:

> . . . that all men are . . . endowed by their Creator with certain unalienable Rights, that among these are Life, Liberty and the pursuit of Happiness.

By proclaiming the Creator as the endower of men's rights, they proclaimed the Creator as sovereign, denying government that ancient and medieval role. Moralists!

Being a moralist also links me with Walter Lunden, F. A. Hayek, Henry Hazlitt, and an encouraging number of other moralists and ethicists of increasing influence. However, this does not mean that all of us see precisely eye to eye. That would be as undesirable as it is impossible. Why? It is our differences that serve as steppingstones to truth, an infinite pursuit. We agree on being moralists, not immoralists, moral values being the correct vantage point from which to look for improvement, refinement. Thus, let each share whatever his best thoughts reveal—the upgrading procedure, that is, learning from each other, catholicity the rule.

What are the foundations of morality? Moralists have varying answers to this question. My foundations are the Golden

---

[1]The belief expressed in this paragraph is not to suggest that I am warranted in breaking laws contrary to this belief. See Chapter 24, "Civil Obedience," in *Talking to Myself* (Irvington-on-Hudson, N.Y.: The Foundation for Economic Education, Inc., 1970), pp. 151-155.

Rule and the Ten Commandments. The Golden Rule, in my view, is the prime tenet of sound economics and, doubtless, the oldest ethical proposition of distinctly universal character. Let no one do to others that which he would not have them do to him; that would be just about the ideal, economically, socially, morally, ethically. Admittedly, this is more a goal than a likelihood, but it is goals we are considering.

There are moral values which are appropriately reinforced by man-made law, and other moral values which do not lend themselves to legal implementation. Let us examine the Ten Commandments to find where man-made laws are appropriate, that is, where they are complementary to the moral law, and where not.

Man-made laws—legal edicts backed by force—are inappropriate when directed at what the individual thinks or believes or does to himself. A man's inner life can only be impaired, never improved, by coercive forces. Government is but an arm of society and its only proper role is to codify and inhibit injuries inflicted on society, that is, on others than self. Self-injury is subject to self-correction—none other!

Take the Commandment, "Thou shalt not covet." Enforce this by a man-made law? The absurdity is obvious. Envy is the root of many evils—stealing, killing, and the like—yet it cannot be done away with by the gun, billy club, fist, or any other physical force. Might as well pass a law against stress or worry or despair or man's thoughts about the here-after or against suicide, for that matter. The you's and I's—society —may lament the ills many people inflict on themselves but we cannot correct them by legal concoctions.

The moralist concedes that there is good and evil in the world—in man—in any man—that there is a moral law by which one may distinguish the good from the evil. But he knows that he is powerless to relieve any individual of the certain consequences of that person's immoral actions. Would he try to enact legislation to the effect that a person shall not be burned if he touches a hot stove or drown if he stays indefinitely under water without air? Such human enactments would be inconsistent with the moral laws of cause and consequence— would indeed be a form of tyranny, an invitation to lawlessness in the mistaken belief that one might violate the moral law with impunity.

Here are a few samplings of government out of bounds, minding your and my business: driving a car without seat belts, staying away from school, working for less than $2.00 an hour, laboring more than 40 hours a week, keeping stores open on the Sabbath, exchanging the fruits of one's labor for gold, on and on. All in the name of protecting the you's and me's against ourselves. Law? Not the way a moralist would define it! These are tyrannies.

Clearly, the moral law takes precedence over the legal edicts of civil law. The latter serves a useful purpose *provided* its limited role is understood and heeded. When statutory law invades the domain of the moral law, it is itself ineffective and it paralyzes moral action; it creates a vacuum.

Coercively enforce an observation of the Golden Rule when only self-enforcement is possible? Nonsensical! Can the government stop covetousness by making it illegal? Of course not! The role of civil law should be limited exclusively to inhibiting such injuries as some inflict on others, never directed at injuries we inflict on ourselves.

My moral code is founded on the Golden Rule and the Ten Commandments, and I would call upon the civil law to help enforce only these: "Thou shalt not kill," "Thou shalt not steal," and "Thou shalt not bear false witness."

Conceded, killing, stealing, and bearing false witness inflict self-injury: the destruction of one's soul, the loss of neighborly respect, the reduction of prospects for cooperation. However, each of these evils inflicts injuries on others and thus becomes a societal problem. Such destructive behavior should be inhibited, insofar as possible, by the organized and legal arm of society—government.

All but the mentally deficient stand against the murder of one by another and more or less agree that one means of minimizing the practice is to oblige the murderer to pay the penalty for his crime.

Mass murder, on the other hand—killings by the millions—is not so much frowned upon. Why? These are done in the name of a collective and thus are thoughtlessly regarded as impersonal. I didn't do it; the nation (or some other abstraction) did it! Witness the Crusades in the name of Christianity or the Thirty Years War in Central Europe, or what goes on more and more in our time.[2] The Commandment, "Thou shalt not kill," is no less broken when done in the name of a collective than when one man kills another. What is the explanation for this calamitous trend? In my view, omnipotent government, that is, government, not the Creator, as sovereign.

Only those who reason clearly from cause to consequence stand foursquare in support of "Thou shalt not steal." True,

---

[2]For further reflection on this complex matter, see my "Conscience on the Battlefield." The Thirty Years War witnessed the slaughter of millions of people "to the glory of God"! See *Grey Eminence* by Aldous Huxley (New York: Harper & Bros., 1941).

not one in a thousand would steal a penny from a child's bank
or a neighbor's goose or another's loaf of bread. Full respect
for private property at the you-and-me level! Yet, people by
the millions will ask the government to do the taking for them
—billions upon billions of dollars annually. Plunder at the impersonal level! Why? The same old reason: government out
of bounds, that is, government as sovereign. "The king can do
no wrong; therefore, what he does for me at the expense of
others is right." Sound reasoning? Hardly!

Those who cherish liberty are well advised to respect and
defend the rightful claims of others. As Santayana wrote,
"The man who is not permitted to own is owned." Observe
that "Thou shalt not steal" presupposes private ownership,
the bedrock or foundation of individual liberty. Why this
assertion? How possibly could one steal were nothing owned!
To disregard this moral law is to deny being one's own man;
disobedience invites enslavement—being owned. Merely observe how the fruits of individual effort are increasingly expropriated by the collective, how our options of ownership are
being diminished. And the way to reverse this dreadful trend
is to heed the Commandment against theft. Government's
role here, as in the case of murder, is to inhibit these infractions of the moral law, not to promote them.

"Thou shalt not bear false witness" means not to misrepre-
sent or defraud or falsify. Make a contract, keep it. Let all
representations be truthful, whether they pertain to persons
or to goods and services. False witness, having to do with
injury to others, rationally warrants that the civil law help
rescue us from this evil.

To my way of thinking, morality, once shattered, destroys
the people and whoever or whatever presumes to rule. It is

only the *consciousness* of moral obligations that binds men together. This is one reason why I am an unabashed moralist and why I hope that our tribe may increase in number and improve in consciousness. Amen!

15

ON BEING MY OWN MAN

Nothing is at last sacred but the integrity of your own mind. Absolve you to yourself, and you shall have the suffrage of the world.

—EMERSON

Emerson's first sentence is clear: be one's own honest self, that is, reflect in word and deed whatever one's highest conscience dictates as righteous. The second, while somewhat obscure, means that if one divorces himself from the integrity of this own mind—responds not to this sacredness—the world will disapprove. In a word, others will see through the sham of one's pretending to stand for every idea in the world but his own.

Should I be my own man? Of course! Should I be your man? Of course not! For confirmation of the point merely ask yourself, should you be my man? The very idea of such voluntary enslavement should be repulsive to any man. And so should the pretense of being everyone's man—or even the majority's man.

93

What is meant by being everyone's man? Examples are all about us: speakers who care not what they say so long as it brings applause; writers of books and articles catering solely to popular demand, be it for pornography, ideological nonsense, or how to feed more bountifully at the government trough; politicians who seek tenure by responding to mass pressures—not each his own but, rather, every voter's man.

I want to examine this political issue further. But first I must point out that there is far more to the good life than just the political side of it. I do not pretend that politics is everything.

With that precaution, my question is this: Is it to the advantage of the citizenry—the voters—to have in political office one who purports to reflect all our diverse views, likes and dislikes, preferences as to what the government should and shouldn't do, the results of opinion polls? Or would it be better for all of us if the successful candidate stood in office, as hopefully in his campaign, for what he believes to be right. Open to economic, moral, and spiritual counsel, yes; but having heard, then acting strictly according to his own best judgment—*within the limits of the law*. Which would be the better man in office?

I know the popular trend is toward the former. But I believe we would fare better with the second kind, a statesman, if I may draw that distinction. Mine is a personal opinion rather than the result of a public opinion poll. Frankly, I have a great faith in the few who insist on being their own true selves and have no trust at all in those who want to be everyone's man.

Let me dramatize the contrast as I see it. The leading politician who claims to be *our* man is like a brilliant leaf in a whirlwind. His is but a reflection of a political potpourri. The candidate I prefer is the one who stands like a rock for what his highest conscience dictates as righteous. I may not agree with where he stands, but let him stand firmly on his own.

I like the way Tolstoy put the idea:

> From the day when the first members of councils placed exterior authority higher than interior, that is to say, recognized the decisions of men united in councils as more important and more sacred than reason and conscience, on that day began lies that caused the loss of millions of human beings and which continue their unhappy work to the present day.

Let us examine "men united in councils" on a small scale— a committee of three. No two are likely to have precisely the same view of what's right and wrong; each has his own unique concept of truth: whatever his reason and highest conscience dictates as righteous. This may not in fact be truth but is as close as any human being can come to truth.

The three, however, have been requested to render a report on what should be done about their rent-controlled city. The first member is devoted to the welfare-state idea and believes that rents should forever be controlled by government. The second member is a devotee of the free market, limited government, private ownership way of life and therefore believes that rent control should be abolished at once. The third member believes rent control to be bad but thinks that the decontrol should be effected gradually, over a period of years.

This is not an uncommon situation, a committee of three men honestly holding three irreconcilable beliefs. Yet, a report is expected of them. What to do? Why not settle on something not too disagreeable to a majority—two of them. What would it be? Heaven only knows! It might read somewhat as follows: Resolved that landlords be permitted to increase rents at an annual rate not to exceed 7.7 per cent.

In this hypothetical but typical instance, the recommendation is a fabrication, pure and simple. Truth, as understood by any one of the three, has no spokesman. By any reasonable definition a lie has been told. The cause of this lie? Members of councils placing exterior authority higher than interior—divorcing themselves from reason and conscience. Tolstoy was right, and so was Charles Kettering when he said, "If you want to kill any idea in the world today, get a committee working on it."

On a matter such as rent control, there would be more than just one organization and its committee at work. More than likely there would be a dozen or so ranging from the League of Women Voters to the Apartment Owner's Association.

Now, assume that the Mayor has the final say on the matter. If he be a politician—*our man*—he will weigh all the lies and render a decision that will, in his opinion, be the least unpopular—the big lie! If, on the other hand, the Mayor be a statesman—*his own man*—he will render a decision which his reason and conscience dictates as right. I'll take the statesman every time and in all situations, local or national. Why? As a voter—any voter—I am more advantaged by the truth than by lies. True, I may not like his decision, but I would rather know where he stands than to know where *he* thinks the rest of us stand.

Move now from small to big scale, from a committee of three to a "committee of the whole," as it is called—in this case all the voters who write and speak and urge their views, yours and mine included. How many "committees of the whole" are there in the U.S.A.? There are more than 100,000 governments in our land, ranging through villages, towns, school districts, counties, states, and nation.

The subjects at issue? Rent control is merely a drop in the bucket. Politico-economic matters under consideration run into the thousands, so many that no officeholder or anyone else can possibly name them all! A mere sampling of the issues: social security, medicare, food stamps and welfare schemes galore, farm subsidies, all forms of transportation including streets, interstate highways and subway systems, foreign and military aid, wage and price controls, minimum wage and maximum hours and other labor matters, aid to education, barriers to trade both domestic and foreign—on and on, seemingly without end. The number of opportunities for committees to fabricate lies staggers the imagination.

To grasp the problem we face, imagine yourself as the head of a state or of the union. Instead of the single problem faced by the Mayor on the relatively minor matter of rent control, you are now confronted with problems so numerous and diverse that no person could ever resolve them intelligently. Have you any idea how to go about solving all the problems of mankind? Of course not! But neither has anyone else that wisdom or capacity.

What then are we to do? Reduce government to the point where no creative activity—not one—comes under its control. Let government—federal, state, and local—confine itself to codifying the taboos—destructive activities—and enforcing such laws. In a word, let government invoke a common justice and keep the peace. That's a whale of a job in itself!

Creative activities? Leave them without exception to men

acting freely, competitively, privately, cooperatively, voluntarily; that is, leave these activities to the free and unfettered market, for it is the market that possesses a wisdom unimaginably greater than exists in any discrete individual.

Each of us—every living person—is, for all practical purposes, more or less a know-nothing, pretenses to the contrary notwithstanding. Therefore, never concede to any human being a wisdom he does not possess or powers over others which he is incapable of exercising beneficially. Let me be my own man—a privilege I would extend to every peaceful person.

16

THE INVISIBLE HAND

*. . . by directing that industry in
such a manner as its produce may
be of the greatest value, he intends
only his own gain, and he is in this,
as in many other cases, led by an*
invisible hand *to promote an end
which was no part of his intention.*
—ADAM SMITH

For years I have quoted this famous line from *The Wealth of
Nations,* but have often wondered precisely what Adam
Smith meant by "invisible hand." The answer is not to be
found in his monumental book. Smith was a moral philosopher, so it is my guess that he referred to the Divine Will,
the order-producing factor in the universe. Invisible? Yes!
Knowable? To some extent! If what I apprehend of the
Divine Will is anywhere near correct, then I am obliged to try
once more to explain the correlation between freedom and
the remarkable outburst of creative energy experienced by the
American people.

If freedom is not seen to be the reason for progress, it may
be neglected and abandoned as of no value. When that happens, we are beset by all sorts of authoritarian controls,
along with shortages and rationing. Does this not justify my
attempt to explain?

The lives of all persons, be they dictocrats or practitioners of the Golden Rule, are identified with self-interest. The differences have to do with how intelligently self-interest is interpreted. The man to whom Adam Smith referred interpreted his self-interest as best served by producing goods or services of the greatest possible value that he might gain the most for himself. In a word, he was minding his own business. He intended nothing more; indeed, like most people then and now, he was utterly unaware of anything more—of consequences beyond his own gain.

However, have a look at the man who minds his own business; for certain, he is not minding anyone else's business. By reason of this fact, no other person is restrained by him. All others, insofar as his actions are concerned, are free men, even though that thought does not occur to him. Just a man tending to his own knitting, oblivious of the beneficial overall effects of such behavior—"led by an invisible hand to promote an end which was no part of his intention."

The end? Clear as crystal: the freedom of everyone to express his uniqueness and seek his own gain! No restraints—none whatsoever—against the release of creative human energy. It is this end and this alone which has accounted for the American miracle.

Adam Smith's man, releasing his own talents and permitting all others to release theirs, acts correctly, ideally. Correct action bears fruits unimaginable in quantity and quality. True, this astounding result is no part of his intention—he intends only his own gain. Further, the freedom which his kind of action assures is beyond the scope of sensory perception; it is not seen with the eyes or heard with the ears. It is in this sense invisible. As in a magnetic field, the forces of attraction are invisible; they cannot be seen or heard; nonetheless, they work. Freedom—its attractive forces likewise invisible—works!

When it is recognized that most people regard as reality only that which comes within the range of their sensory perceptions, it becomes clear why invisible freedom is so rarely correlated with human progress. The progress they observe is credited instead to what they can see or feel or hear: coercive gadgetry such as compulsory unionism, social security, medicare, socialized mail delivery, government education, dilution of the money supply, wage and price controls, rationing and, to top it off, national self-sufficiency, isolationism, call it what you will. Few, indeed, are those who realize that it is the attractive force of invisible freedom that accounts *exclusively* for whatever progress there is or ever will be.

It would be very well if Adam Smith's economic man would persist in his ways—"by directing that industry in such a manner as its produce may be of the greatest value, he intends only his own gain." He would, in this circumstance, "be led by an invisible hand to promote an end which was no part of his intention." But that man, to whom freedom is invisible, is the very one who, more than likely, is drawn off course, who correlates what is visible to him with the progress he observes. Unwittingly, he joins the interventionist parade, seeking gain not by improving his own industry but by trying to seize the fruits of the industry of others. Blindly, he becomes his own worst enemy. Adam Smith, be it noted, spoke of what-ought-to-be, rather than what-is.

Thank heaven, there are two ways of seeing. True, no one can see freedom with his eyes or hear it with his ears. Freedom, in this sense, is invisible. Were this the only way of seeing, the case for freedom would be hopeless. No one would ever correlate progress with men acting freely. All would be lost!

The other way of seeing? *Insight,* with which a few are graced and many others could be.

Insight, rather than the outward, superficial glimpse of things and events, is an inward, behind-the-scenes observation—"the ability to understand and see clearly the inner nature of things." It is achieved, if at all, by reflecting on what one sees when looking under the covers, so to speak, for causal sequences. Perhaps such insights can be attributed to interceptions of the Divine Will. But without resort to mysticism, we do know that seekers after light experience more insights than nonseekers. "Seek and ye shall find," so it was said of old; and it is true today.

However, one does not need to reflect very deeply to see why all progress stems from individuals acting creatively as they freely choose without violating the right of others to do likewise. Merely assess your own life. Is it not obvious that no other could identify your uniqueness, be he acclaimed the wisest who ever lived. Adam Smith comments on this:

> The statesman who should attempt to direct private people in what manner they ought to employ their capitals would not only load himself with a most unnecessary attention, but assume an authority which could safely be trusted, not only to no single person, but to no council or senate whatever, and which would nowhere be so dangerous as in the hands of a man who had folly and presumption enough to fancy himself fit to exercise it.

Further, so far as you are concerned, whoever you may be, all insights, flashes of intuition, discoveries, inventions are exclusively personal outcroppings; these enlightenments never have been nor can they be the coercive impositions of any other person. Insights are not implants but outgrowths of the inner self.

Freedom, while invisible to the eye that only looks outward, is clearly and easily visible to the eye that can and does see within. Freedom undeniably has the case. What is lacking is the insight.

Of course, ever so many people in today's world will look down upon Adam Smith's man who "intends only his own gain." They will charge that he is devoid of social consciousness, and so he may be; but not of social behavior. William Graham Sumner possessed the insight to reveal this apparent contradiction.

Every man and woman in society has one big duty. That is, to take care of his or her own self. This is a social duty. For, fortunately, the matter stands so that the duty of making the best of one's self individually is not a separate thing from the duty of filling one's place in society, but the two are one, and the latter is accomplished when the former is done.[1]

Freedom is indeed the invisible hand, the magnetic force that draws to the use of each the unique talents of everyone. As a part of this mysterious attractive force which governs the whole universe, it is not a surface thing for outward observation. Further, even those who see "the inner nature of things" do not know precisely *what* it is; they do, however, know *that* it is—and they know of the magic it works. May their tribe increase, for to the bounties of freedom there is no end.

---

[1]William Graham Sumner, *What Social Classes Owe To Each Other* (Caldwell, Idaho: Caxton Printers, 1954) p. 98.

17

FROM INSTINCT TO
REASON TO INSIGHT

*A moment's insight is sometimes
worth a life's experience.*

—O. W. HOLMES

It is obvious that Dr. Holmes had his own moments of insight—man's highest and rarest experience—or else he could never have written that profound line.

Is there a way for each of us to glimpse such moments? It is my conviction that there is such a way, and here, at the outset, is a summary of my thesis: All animal behavior is governed by instinct; human behavior is more conformable to instinct than is generally thought to be the case; reason or unreason improves or subverts instinct; insight is a potentiality of the human being and, though extremely rare in actuality, it can replace instinct to man's emergence and glory. Can this sequence of behavioral qualities be supported by reason? That's the question! If so, we can better set our sights aright.

The definitions:

- *Instinct* is "an inborn tendency to behave in a way characteristic of a species."
- *Reason* is "the ability to think, form judgments, draw conclusions."
- *Insight* is "the ability to see and understand clearly the inner nature of things."

I agree with the above observation about insight by Dr. Holmes and also Edward Young's thoughts on instinct and reason:

Reason is progressive; instinct is complete; swift instinct leaps; slow reason feebly climbs.

Yes, we have the dictionary definitions. But what, really, is instinct? While most of us know what instinct does, not one knows what it is. The same goes for reason. And, as to insight, the experience is so rare that only a few even know that it is, let alone what it is.

Why should anyone speculate on procedures for progressing from instinct, which is so prevalent in life, to reason, which is more an aspiration than a reality, and then on to insight which is rarely even an aspiration? Perhaps by speculation we can arrive at an improved understanding of our personal and societal problems and how better to resolve them. We should everlastingly try to discover the true path to our destiny and edge toward it. And this we can do through insight, a rarity akin to the proverbial needle in the haystack. Conceded, we can do no better than to generalize on prevalence and rarity; these traits can never be quantified.

As to life governed by instinct, it ranges all the way from microscopic plankton through vast variations and gradations to insects, fish, birds, chimps, horses, dogs, extending to a marked extent into the human race. In a word, instinct rules all organic life, including an enormous proportion of mankind's behavior.

In glorifying rare insight, we should not denigrate prevalent instinct. How wondrous this is to behold! For instance: whence comes the ant's gift of knowing she must bite every grain of corn she buries in her hill so it will not take root and grow? Who taught the salmon to return to its birthplace for spawning? Asked Bacon, "Who taught the bee to fly through such a vast sea of air and to find the way from a flower in a field to her hive?" How do geese find their way from here to there and back again? All a mysterious gift of Creation—instinct!

Based on observing self and others, my opinion is that instinct plays no less a role in human beings than in animals. Conceding this unprovable assumption, what, then, is the distinction between animal and human behavior as related to instinct?

Man is the highest form of life, separate and apart from all the forms below. In what way apart? Man alone has the power to choose, to will his own actions, to think for himself. Only man has the *potentiality* of reasoning, of hindsight, foresight, insight. Thus man, in contrast to other forms of life, shapes his own destiny. And the historical record makes it plain that he, unlike the birds and bees, does not go unerringly to his destination but errs in countless ways. Man is gifted with a freedom of choice so powerful and radical that he can deny his Creator; thus man, not Creation, is, for the time being, in command of his behaviors. Estimations of man range all the way from "How like an angel!" to "Nature's

wayward son." That these appraisals apply to all of us, more
or less, seems obvious.

Nature's wayward son: Several philosophers whose judgments I respect suggest that man has lost most of the instincts
that govern animal behavior; and he has failed, to a marked
extent, to acquire the higher traits that should govern human
behavior. I agree with the conclusion but not the analysis.
What, then, is my suspicion?

Here it is: Instincts endow the animal with internal guidelines, while in man these directional signals are subject to
his manipulation. Man, in other words, has the power to will
his own actions, but being distressingly short on reason and
insight, he tends to pervert his natural instincts for survival.
He turns his instincts against himself. Among the lower or-
ders, it is instinct which deters these creatures from killing
their own kind. Honey bees rarely kill honey bees; robins do
not kill robins; a wolf never kills a wolf. Scavengers on occasion, yes, but seldom does this order of creation evidence
cannibalism. Man? There are a few who will kill and eat each
other—cannibals—but there are untold numbers of humans
who slaughter our own species by the millions—and "think"
nothing of it! That is, they do not reason; rather, these people, by the absence of reason and insight, subvert instinct
from a survival attribute to a self-annihilating trait.

There is no need to labor this point. Merely reflect on the
countless ways human beings in every nation on this earth
fail to identify their actions with intelligent self-interest, and
there you have examples of instinct perverted by man's power
to will into actuality his own short-sightedness. Nature's wayward son, indeed.

How like an angel! This exclamation by Shakespeare assuredly did not refer to the mill run of Englishmen or to any other nationality of his or any other period. No political or economic power monger, no perpetrator of or participant in religious wars, could ever inspire such an accolade as "angel."

Nor was the reference to man's ability to teach and learn from each other, remarkable and widespread as is this talent. True, man teaches and absorbs everything from the three R's to history and philosophy. We can teach animals, from dogs to insects—remember "the flea circus"? Indeed, the higher animals teach their offspring.

For these reasons, I am beginning to believe that the teacher-learner procedure falls in the instinctual category. The dam, for instance, seems not to err in teaching her puppies. Instinct guides her aright. Man, however, in imposing his imperfect reason on this natural instinct, errs in countless ways. It is this linkage of ignorance and instinct that accounts for all the nonsense that is "taught and listened to." What, then, could the Bard of Avon have had in mind?

Shakespeare could have had nothing less in mind than those rarest of all human attributes: reason and insight—the few flickers of the angelic in mankind. He had these phenomena in mind because his own mind was so obviously graced with reason and insight. Few have ever written with greater wisdom and perspicacity.

"Reason is progressive . . . slow reason feebly climbs." In contrast to this truth, an individual of uncommon brilliance remarked to me, "I am the completely rational person." It is to laugh! To repeat from a previous chapter, Socrates knew better: "I know nothing." Compared to the Infinite Unknown he was right. Montaigne knew better. Inscribed on his coat of arms was *Que sais-je*—What do I know? The eminent economist, Ludwig von Mises, knew better. Even I, along with a host of others, know better.

Reason is, at best, progressive; it feebly climbs when and if it ever does. There never has been nor will there ever be a completely rational person. Pure reason is infinitely beyond the reach of finite minds. The cure for this little god syndrome? A humility that squares with reality. Short of this, feeble reason warps, distorts, subverts man's instincts.

Finally, as to rare insights. Is there a guideline, a way that each of us may be so graced, more or less? The search, surely, is worth the effort for, as Dr. Holmes so wisely observed, "A moment's insight is sometimes worth a life's experience." In a word, it is worthwhile to strive for just one of those rare moments. By so doing, several such moments might follow.

Based on what I have observed among those who experience insights, the eye looks never downward but only heavenward, that is, toward the Infinite Unknown. Each truth gleaned—enlightenment—is an insight and gives off a glow, the more insights one possesses the brighter is the beam he radiates. This light cannot see us but those who have eyes to see can see it and be brightened accordingly. Nor is this a momentary glow; it is potentially everlasting. Otherwise, how account for Confucius, Moses, Socrates, Epictetus, Shakespeare, to name but a few mortals whose insights are immortal! We have life by reason of insights, that is, if we know how to distinguish the true among them from the false. Why this observation?

There is evidence aplenty that even these rare persons who peer into the unknown, sometimes glimpse error and believe it to be truth. Thus, those of us who get our insights secondhand must find a way of forming our own judgments. Are these ideas true or false? How, pray tell, can we know?

Let me share my way. If someone's "insight" suggests that he or any other imperfect person—whoever among erring mankind—shall dominate or rule one or more of his fellowmen, it is patently false.

Insights that reveal truth always relate to the freeing, releasing, unmasking of the human spirit. Glimpses of Creation —intuitive flashes—if seen correctly, are in harmony with liberty and individual creativity; they are, without exception, lessons on how to grow, emerge, evolve, develop in awareness, perception, consciousness.

The key to unlocking this highest of all human resources, that is, if there be one? Based on my reading, observations, reflections, the secret is dedicated *conscious* effort, nothing less than the passionate pursuit of excellence.

These, I believe, are appropriate guidelines—the way, eventually, to replace man's distorted instincts with insights, to edge toward human destiny: individuals ascending toward enlightenment.

18

BITING THE HAND
THAT FEEDS*

*We set ourselves to bite the hand
that feeds us.*

—EDMUND BURKE

The above line by Edmund Burke, written in 1770, had, I feel certain, reference to a common trait: ingratitude—and not to the hand I have in mind. The "hand" he had critically in mind was revealed to him 25 years later:

And having looked to *government* for bread, on the very first scarcity they will turn and bite the hand that fed them.

Government in Burke's day was popularly regarded—but not by Burke—as the hand that fed. Adam Smith's great work, *The Wealth of Nations*, published in the period between Burke's two statements, had not as yet penetrated very many minds.

While ingratitude is doubtless a trait as common as ever, it

---

*This chapter originally appeared as an article in the medical magazine, *Private Practice*, Oklahoma City.

is no more responsible for today's "biting the hand that feeds" than it was in the days of mercantilism. What then? An abysmal ignorance of what the real hand is! How can people be expected to pay homage and respect to something if they know nothing of its existence? What is to keep them from looking to fictitious "hands" and, by so doing, biting the unseen hand, the only one that feeds? Nothing can put them on the right track but enlightenment, an illumination so bright that they cannot help but see the real hand!

As I read and study the succeeding issues of *Private Practice,* and note the succession of meat and fuel and paper and other recurrent crises that plague us today, it seems more important than ever that all of us—and especially the professional healers of physical and mental disturbances—come to a better appreciation of the real helping hand in human affairs.

The late eminent scholar, Dr. Thomas Nixon Carver, Professor of Political Economy at Harvard for 32 years, remarked to me, "The two most important books in Western Civilization are the Holy Bible and *The Wealth of Nations."*

No need for me to defend the Bible, nor should the Industrial Revolution set in motion by Adam Smith's monumental work require more defense than it has had.[1] Nevertheless, it does! No movement beneficial to the millions has been more effectively maligned or had more derogatory assessments and false interpretations than the Industrial Revolution. Were the truth known, the real hand would be revealed.

I would not suggest that *Capitalism and the Historians* be

---

[1]It is almost certain that Adam Smith had no idea, when writing *The Wealth of Nations,* that the Industrial Revolution would be a by-product thereof. He had some good ideas that took root and flourished.

required reading in or out of school, any more than "coke" should be required drinking![2] Instead, we might hope that it be *desired* reading by all seekers of truth whatever their age. This enlightening book gives the details of those early years of the Industrial Revolution for all who care to know; it exposes the untruths that have been written by "historians." Here, however, I shall give only the highlights.

Reflect on the economic situation in the British Isles prior to the year 1800. Wrote Adam Smith, "It is not uncommon, I have been frequently told, in the Highlands of Scotland for a mother who has borne twenty children not to have two alive." In a word, the infant mortality rate was so high that only a small percentage of the population reached adulthood.

Wealth? It was mansions, paintings, jewels and servants—serfs—galore.

To whom did producers cater? To Lords of the Manor and the like—the "wealthy."

Reflect on the current economic situation in the British Isles, the U.S.A., and several other countries—outgrowths of the Industrial Revolution.

The infant, adolescent, and adult mortality rate has markedly declined. The average life expectancy is now around 70 years. A mother can count on virtually all of her children outliving her.

Wealth? It has for decades been goods and/or services in a million and one forms.[3] Literally thousands of Americans who would have been serfs two centuries ago are now mil-

---

[2]*Capitalism and the Historians,* edited by F. A. Hayek. Chicago: University of Chicago Press, Phoenix Books, 1963.

[3]General Electric, for instance, one among countless producers, manufactures more than 200,000 different products.

lionaires. Today's wage earners are wealthier than any Lord of the Manor ever was.

To whom do present-day producers cater? To the masses, young and old alike. What customers want, producers supply —ranging from diapers and toys to soaps, paper tissues, sanitary facilities, gas and electric stoves and lighting, dishwashers, TV sets, autos, travel by air, or whatever; the list of what composes real wealth is endless!

Who are these producers? The ones who, only a few decades earlier, would have been serfs.

What was the main outcropping of the Industrial Revolution which brought in its train the greatest and most beneficial economic changes in the world's history? It was freedom, the freedom of *anyone* to be his creative self; the freedom to exchange with whomever he pleased; the freedom to seek his own gain so long as he did it peacefully.

The very individuals, who in Adam Smith's time would have been serfs, were free to go as far as their aspirations and talents would take them. Once these so-called commoners were unshackled, their blindfolds removed—unmasked— their hidden potentialities literally burst forth. From these heretofore lowly folk emerged scientists, inventors, entrepreneurs, philosophers, educators, poets, and literary figures. Such names as Marconi and Einstein; Whitney, Edison, Bell and McCormick; Leland Stanford, Carnegie, Ford, Sloan, and the Wright brothers; Bastiat, Booker T. Washington, Andrew Dixon White, Mises, Alfred North Whitehead, T. S. Eliot—and countless thousands of others, many born in poverty and rising to the top. The freeing of the human spirit! In a word, the free and unfettered market—at least its nearest approximation in all time.

Doubtless it was from observing phenomena of this kind that the eminent psychiatrist, Dr. Fritz Kunkel, was inspired to write:

> Immense hidden powers lurk in the unconscious of the most common man—indeed, of all people without exception.

What then is the hand that feeds? While generally unrecognized, it is seemingly obvious: the free and unfettered market. This is what it is and nothing else!

The point is simply this: Any person who is a party to any infringement of the free and unfettered market is biting the hand that feeds. There are no exceptions. A few samples:

- All coercive work stoppages, such as strikes, "job-actions": To the extent that individuals are removed from productive effort, to that extent are they economic nobodies. The larder of supplies, which alone can fulfill our demands, is not as full as it would otherwise be.
- All coercive exchange stoppages: trade barriers, be they tariffs, embargoes, or exclusive market positions: cartels. This is Lord-of-the-Manor monopoly. Those who would compete, on the basis of their efficiency, are not permitted to do so.
- All coercive pricing, such as wage and price controls: Unless the rewards for goods and services are allowed to be freely set by consumer preferences, producers have no performance guidelines. What ought or ought not to be done cannot be judged from the record. In the absence of such information activity declines. The hand that really feeds is severely bitten.
- All coercive welfarism, be it social security, medicare, unemployment insurance, or the thousands of make-

work projects such as the Gateway Arch, moon shots, urban renewal, public housing. Every one of these is rooted in the fallacious notion of Edmund Burke's time: government is the hand that feeds.

First, the government feeds no one except as it coercively takes the feed from others. And, second, this process withdraws enormous amounts of capital from productive uses, diverting it to nonproduction and mass idleness. It makes commoners out of potentially creative individuals.

I repeat, it is not ingratitude that presently causes most Americans to bite the hand that feeds. It is, instead, a blindness as to what the real hand is. How are we to account for this?

I was brought up in the horse-and-buggy days. We put blinders on our horses so they could see only where we wanted them to go. This is precisely what men are now doing to men— putting blinders on them. All sorts of prestigious persons in politics, business, education, and religion, blind themselves to the hand that feeds, want us to go the only way they see: a dictocratic society—dictocrats at the top, with the rest of us doing their bidding. A return to mercantilism!

The remedy? Remove the blinders and look around on one's own. A modicum of unfettered observation will bring the free and unfettered market into view so clearly that any intelligent person will wonder why he had not seen before the real hand that feeds. Bite it? Never again!

19

THE SANCTIFYING
OF PLUNDER

*The law . . . has converted plunder
into a right, in order to protect
plunder.*

—BASTIAT

The commandment, "Thou shalt not steal," would be far
better kept today had not theft assumed various disguises
under which its practice has been generally sanctified. The
gilding of an evil gives it a virtuous face—a Mr. Hyde's ugli-
ness covered by a comely Dr. Jekyll mask. Why such subter-
fuge? To be thought of as a thief by others or to so regard
oneself is utterly revolting to all but stunted mentalities; so,
we try to sanctify our plunder!

The sanctification of plunder is as old as the history of man.
If thievery was indeed the first labor-saving device, it was developed out of sheer ignorance. Survival is a laudable objective; therefore, if thievery is thought to be the only means to
that good end, it must perforce be good. Thus is plunder
sanctified by those who know no better.

117

Many tribal societies have practiced plunder, raiding their neighbors, taking home all the loot they could garner. But we can hardly be critical of them without criticizing ourselves.

Perhaps no other book has more wisdom between its covers than the Holy Bible. Yet, we find written there about twenty-three centuries ago: "Men do not despise a thief, if he steals to satisfy his soul when he is hungry."[1] This was written centuries later than "Thou shalt not steal." How can any practice be more sanctified than by biblical endorsement! However, we must understand the times lest we render too harsh a judgment.

Move on another fifteen centuries to St. Thomas Aquinas:

> The superfluities of the rich belong by right to the poor. . . . To use the property of another, taking it secretly in case of extreme need, cannot, properly speaking, be characterized as theft.[2]

Seven centuries ago, at the time of Aquinas, who were the rich? They were plunderers, the feudal lords who lived off the serfs—the poor. In all justice, what the lords possessed belonged less to them than to the serfs from whom they had taken it. Considering the politico-economic darkness in medieval times, it is understandable how a religious leader might sanctify plunder by those who had been plundered. The axiom, "Thou shalt not steal," was but an ancient flash of light with no sustaining source of energy.

There is no need for further illustrations of plunder sanctified. Every age and all civilizations abound with examples

---

[1] Proverbs 6:30 (King James version). It might be noted that modern translations render this passage differently.

[2] See Thomas Aquinas, 2a, 2ae, quaestiao 66, art. 7.

of this primitive trait of gilding evil that it may appear virtuous, a weakness which prevails to this day. There were some excuses in times past, prior to a knowledge of free market phenomena. But what of the present? How do we now sanctify plunder?

Today, whichever way the majority votes is generally conceded to be the criterion for what's right and wrong.[3] Once this nonsensical foundation of morality is accepted—approval by the majority—plunder is legalized and thus sanctified. Legislation, being a collective action, leaves hardly anyone with a sense of guilt. Why? The evil is depersonalized. Comparable is the mob that hangs Joe Doakes. The mob did it! The truth? Each of the lynchers committed the murder precisely as each person who is a party to legal plunder is guilty. Yet, the collective action affords each participant a false sense of absolution.

Legal plunder in the U.S.A. today, in dollar amount, is many thousands of times greater than, say, at the time of Aquinas or even during the lives of our founding fathers. In those days someone stole a pig or chicken or some other small item, not because thieves were more scrupulous then than now but simply because no one owned very much. However, my guess is that the proportion of all private property which is stolen or plundered is substantially the same today as in the past. What has changed, aside from the method of sanctification? The total quantity of property owned is thousands of times greater now than before. There is incomparably more to plunder, that's all. The propensity to plunder—to live off the

---

[3]For an excellent analysis of this fallacy, see "The American System and Majority Rule," by The Reverend Edmund A. Opitz. *The Freeman*, November 1962.

fruits of the labor of others—appears to be as persistent a trait as it is evil.

In the light of free market, private ownership, limited government practices with their moral and spiritual antecedents —of which the American people have had a remarkable sampling—how is this possible? I am now beginning to understand. This way of life has been but a flash of enlightenment, as dimly perceived as "Thou shalt not steal." The freedom philosophy, with but few exceptions, is no better understood than was the commandment against theft of more than thirty centuries ago. No intellectual muscle in either case, no sustaining force.

With few exceptions, the masses of people in this and other "advanced" countries have not correlated the fantastic outburst of creative energy with the practice of freedom. Ortega pinpoints this failure:

> The world which surrounds the new man from his birth does not compel him to limit himself in any fashion, it sets up no veto in opposition to him, on the contrary, it incites his appetite, which in principle can increase indefinitely. Now it turns out—and this is most important—that this world of the XIXth and early XXth centuries not only has the perfections and the completeness which it actually possesses, but furthermore suggests to those who dwell in it the radical assurance that tomorrow it will be still richer, ampler, more perfect, as if it enjoyed a spontaneous, inexhaustible power of increase. . . . They believe in this as they believe the sun will rise in the morning. The metaphor is an exact one. For, in fact, the common man, finding himself in a world so excellent, technically and socially, believes it has been produced by nature, and never thinks of the per-

sonal efforts of highly endowed individuals which the creation of this new world presupposed. *Still less will he admit the notion that all these facilities still require the support of certain difficult human virtues, the least failure of which would cause the rapid disappearance of the whole magnificent edifice.*[4] (Italics added)

Is there a remedy? Yes, but the price gives the appearance of being too high. First, there is required of you and me a far better understanding of the freedom philosophy than we now possess and, to top it off, brilliant explanations of its efficacy. In a word, show the correlation between the abundant life and freedom so attractively that others are bound to take heed. Actually, this is not a high price—it is the very least we should do for ourselves, if not for others.

Second, let us begin to call this practice of "robbing selected Peter to pay for collective Paul" by its right name: legalized plunder. Frederic Bastiat gave us the measuring rod more then a century ago in *The Law:*

> See if the law takes from some persons what belongs to them, and gives it to other persons to whom it does not belong. See if the law benefits one citizen at the expense of another *by doing what the citizen himself cannot do without committing a crime.* (Italics added)

This question of legal plunder must be settled once and for all, and there are only three ways to settle it:

1—The few plunder the many.
2—Everybody plunders everybody.
3—Nobody plunders anybody.

We must make our choice among limited plunder, uni-

---

[4]From *Revolt of the Masses* by Jose Ortega y Gasset (New York: W. W. Norton & Co., 1932).

versal plunder, and no plunder. The law can follow only one of these three.

Finally, there must be a recognition that might—majority rule—does not make right. Counting noses is no way to decide moral, ethical, or economic matters. This accomplished, plunder will lose its legal backing and, thus, its sanctification.

Let the law defend the rightful owner of property rather than the thief. Let freedom prevail!

20

TRUST THYSELF—
SOME OTHERS DO

*Trust men and they will be true to
you.*

—EMERSON

Based on my experiences over the past forty years, meeting
with and lecturing before countless thousands, it is a safe
guess that 99 percent of the adult population in America today believe in more governmental control over citizens than
I do. These millions would say that I go too far in suggesting
the limits that should be placed on political power.

In other words, *I believe more in those millions than they
believe in themselves!* Farfetched? It all depends on how we
stake out the limits—role, scope—of government.

One cannot logically decide on what government should
and should not do without a precise definition of what government is. I agree with Professor Woodrow Wilson when he
wrote in 1900: "And the authority of governors, directly or
indirectly, rests in all cases ultimately on *force*. Government,
in its last analysis, is organized force."[1] That this is a *physical*

---

[1]See *The State* by Woodrow Wilson (Boston: D. C. Heath & Co., 1900),
p. 572.

force is easy enough to comprehend. Each edict is backed by a constabulary—obey or take the consequences.

If one understands the nature of physical force, he will know what government should and should not do—not necessarily what it will and will not do. Here, we are interested only in what is right.

First, what can physical force do? It can inhibit, prohibit, restrain, penalize. The next logical question is, what should be restrained and penalized? The answer is to be found in the moral codes, many more ancient than Christianity, which condemn such destructive actions of men as fraud, violence, stealing, predation, misrepresentation and the like. This is what physical force can *constructively* do and all it can do; it can enforce the codified moral taboos. Period!

Second, what is it that physical force cannot do? It cannot be a creative force. The creative force, in every instance, is spiritual in the sense that ideas, insights, intuition, inventions, discoveries are spiritual.

> Production is a spiritual, intellectual, and ideological phenomenon. It is the method that man, directed by reason, employs for the best possible removal of uneasiness. What distinguishes our conditions from those of our ancestors who lived one thousand or twenty thousand years ago is not something material but something spiritual. The material changes are the outcome of spiritual changes.[2]

We can deduce from this that all creative activity stems from individuals, for only individuals have ideas, thoughts,

---

[2]Ludwig von Mises, *Human Action* (Chicago: Henry Regnery Company, Third Revised Edition, 1966), p. 142.

insights. Creative men and women are not and cannot be induced to respond creatively to the gun or sword or the threat of violence. The notion that I can command you to have a constructive, creative idea is absurd.

How, then, do we draw the line? How do we stake out the limits of government? As an arm of society, it has no role to play except as the legal, organized extension of those rights which exist in each citizen, namely, the right to defend life, livelihood, and personal freedom, the protector against all destructive actions. Its role is exclusively negative.

But what about the positive? If government—physical force—is ruled out as the stimulator, director, manager of constructive and creative activities, to whom are such activities left? Our answer: to individuals acting voluntarily, cooperatively, competitively, privately—as they freely choose. Government's role can be likened to that of an umpire: to see that there is a fair field and no favors, that no special privilege is extended to anyone—not one!

Why my contention that 99 percent of adult Americans think I go too far in staking out the limits of government power? Except for out-and-out communists or socialists—there are countless thousands of these in the U.S.A. today wearing other labels—99 percent of the remaining citizens will *more or less* agree with my position. However, most everyone insists on an exception; they "leak" here or there, that is, they have a "but" that pleads a special privilege for themselves that only an omnipotent government can bestow. Let government stay within bounds—except to serve them—is what it amounts to![3] Ideological partners—almost!

---

[3] "To serve them" includes forcing others to gratify their charitable feelings—support of government welfare programs and the like.

These "leaks," however, give the case away. It puts the "leakers" on the other side. One "but" endorses the principle of omnipotent government no less than two "buts" or a thousand. What could be more irrational than the notion that one should feather his own nest at the expense of others but let not others feather their nests with what is mine?

Trust thyself—some others do! Who are these others? We do not know precisely, only that they are among the tens of thousands who have more faith in free men than in fettered men. We trust the 99 percent more than they trust themselves! What is meant by this? They do not go all the way in trusting themselves as free and self-responsible citizens. We trust them, as such, all the way. They harbor a fear that they could not thrive without some governmental largesse—plunder. We would replace that fear with the confidence that these millions, acting freely, cooperatively, competitively, voluntarily, privately would maximize their chances of success. We are far more on the side of their true self-interest than they are!

What is our unconventional behavior that causes these people to claim we go too far in limiting political power? It is an attempt at disciplined, consistent thinking, quite contrary to the current mode: Adhere strictly to an ideal that Immanuel Kant called *good will.* The meaning Kant attached to this phrase needs explanation. By "will" he meant the individual's ability rationally to will his own actions. But the word "good" is the key: the adjective "good" can be used—said Kant—only if the principle of universality can be applied to one's maxims.[4]

---

[4]See *Foundations of the Metaphysics of Morals* by Immanuel Kant (Indianapolis: Bobbs-Merrill Company, 1959).

A sample maxim may help to clarify Kant's point, to remove the obscurity: I have the right to my life, livelihood, liberty. Is that a good maxim? According to Kant, only if one can rationally concede that identical right to all other mortal beings—universality. Can I? Yes! Therefore, the maxim is good.

Reverse the maxim: I have the right to take the life, livelihood, liberty of another. Good? Only if I can rationally concede the right of murder, theft, enslavement to all living mortals. Can I? Indeed, not! Therefore, it is not good.

The charge that we "go too far" because we are too consistent is not a valid criticism, in my view. Should not every person at least try to be consistent?

How can one be consistent in an inconsistent world—contradictions galore? Bear in mind that we have only the choice of living in the world as it is or not living at all. If one chooses to live, he must engage in all sorts of activities at odds with his beliefs, that go against the grain; he is committed to live here and now, however absurd the situation may appear to him. He cannot possibly live the consistent life.

Reflect on those of us who "go too far" in limiting dictatorial power, and the thousands of ways in which our ideal is thwarted. For example, take just one of these infractions: socialized mail, anathema of the first order. Yet, we live with it, use it. In a word, we live inconsistently.

Where, then, are we to find the sole opportunity for practicing the consistent life? *In our proclaimed positions!* We can stand ramrod straight in our written and spoken opposition by demonstrating the efficacy of mail delivery were it left to the free market, that is, to men acting voluntarily, competitively, cooperatively, privately. We can explain that our inefficient mail service is as good as it is despite, not because of, its political authoritarianism; that every item that gets delivered stems from a leakage of free human energy and none—not one item—by reason of the "service's" dictatorial power.

We can proclaim what we believe to be right even though we must live with what we are certain is wrong. This is how to be consistent and no one can be too consistent.

Anyone who consistently stands for the freedom philosophy trusts the exception-makers more than they trust themselves. Their road leads to all-out statism, which would destroy them as free and self-responsible individuals. The road of the freedom devotees, on the other hand, opens the way to all persons to become their potentially creative selves. Trust thyself, not dictocrats! No one else who ever lived can manage your life as well as you can. No one can achieve life's purpose by remote control.

21

AIM TO BE A SEER

In the works of man, as in those of
nature, it is really the motives
which chiefly merit attention.
                    —GOETHE

To live the aimless life is to spend this mortal moment with
the undiscovered self; it is to exist in an obstructed universe,
below the human potential—breathing, but intellectually and
spiritually dormant! Woe to individuals thus afflicted; pity
upon them—and upon any society over which they rule. The
free society is out of the question without a predominance
of mental and spiritual activity. So, as Goethe suggests, let
us look to our motives. In the absence of those whose aim is
to walk in the way of truth, our society is doomed.

Why aim to be a seer? The reason is suggested by one of
the all-time greats, Leonardo da Vinci:

. . . people fall into three classes: Those who see [seers],
those who see when shown, and those who do not see.

Thomas Alva Edison also found three classes of people:

Five percent of the people think, ten percent of the people

129

think they think; and the other eighty-five percent would rather die than think.

As background for my thesis, let me cite two other seers:

That man thinks he knows everything, whereas he knows nothing. I, on the other hand, know nothing, but I know I know nothing.

—SOCRATES

We lie in the lap of immense intelligence, which makes us receivers of its truth and organs of its activity. When we discern justice, when we discern truth, we do nothing of ourselves, but allow a passage of its beams.

—EMERSON

For my own edification, more than for that of others, I shall apply my own value judgments to these observations in the above order. The far-from-wise assessing the far-wiser!

Leonardo speaks of "those who see when shown." Who is it that can point the way for them? The seers, that is, the Leonardos past and present, those gifted with superior understanding along this or that line of thought relative to the rest of humanity.

It is important to recognize that even Leonardo possessed a finite mind, as do we all. He saw but an infinitesimal part of Infinite Truth. This giant, however, was far ahead of most others along the numerous lines of his uniqueness—for instance, foreseeing flying machines and drawing designs of them five centuries ago!

If we can see when shown, what quality must we possess to spot the seers out front? It is precisely the same quality that earmarks the seers: ". . . drawn by the unrealized toward

realization . . . toward clarification, toward consciousness."[1]
When we are thus sensitized, the pacesetters, the exemplars
come within our scope. Seekers respond to the magnetism of
the seer, whoever, wherever, or whenever he may be.

Note that Leonardo's third class is composed of "those who
do not see," rather than those who *cannot* see. This is a hope-
ful view; it is possible for anyone to see, even though many
never do.

Edison, a profound thinker and possibly the greatest inventive genius of all time, when asked from whence his ideas
came, replied, "They come as if from out of the blue." Many
creative individuals have made the identical acknowledg-
ment, implying that their minds were attuned or receptive to
some higher intelligence.

The "Wizard of Menlo Park" divided people into three
classes, as did Leonardo. But Edison presumed to count
noses, that is, he applied percentages to each class. In the
light of the wisdom he intercepted, I must conclude that this
resort to numbers was mere hyperbole—"exaggeration for
effect; not to be taken seriously." For surely those who think
—seers—and those who think they think, and those who would
rather die than think, are self-determined rather than subject
to census by anyone else—not even by Edison.

From whence come these all-time greats? The answer
given by Professor N. J. Berrill, eminent zoologist, holds out
hopes for each of us:

These [Leonardo da Vinci and others] are uncommon
giants, I fully realize, but they are giants who grew out of
the so-called common stock of a multitude of uncommon

[1]See *The Creative Process,* edited by Brewster Ghiselin (New York: A
Mentor Book, New American Library, 1952), p. 18.

individuals of lesser stature. They stand as symbols of the creative individuality of human beings. . . .[2]

As to inventive genius in general, reflect on the following: ". . . the father of photography was an army officer; and of the electric motor, a book-binder's clerk. The inventor of the telegraph was a portrait painter; and of the jacquard loom, a dressmaker. A farmer invented the typewriter; a poet, the sewing machine; a cabinet-maker, the cotton gin; and a coal miner, the locomotive. The telephone was the after-school work of a teacher of the deaf; the disc talking machine, the night work of a clothing salesman; the wax cylinder phonograph, of a lawyer's clerk; the typesetting machine, a grocery-man. A physician made the first pneumatic tire because his little son was an invalid. The story of nearly every great invention has been the result of some one riding a hobby."[3]

What does the author, John Williams, mean in this context by "riding a hobby"? What is the other phrasing? Pursuing one's uniqueness! Discovering one's self! This is the route to becoming a seer, a path blazed by Edison and countless others.

Socrates referred to himself as a philosophical midwife. Why would he assume so modest a role? Whence his reputation for being one of the wisest men who ever lived, although he claimed to know nothing? A seer, yes; but wise enough to claim no credit for it.

This Athenian idealist philosopher and teacher never

---

[2]See *Inherit the Earth* by N. J. Berrill (New York: Dodd, Mead & Company, 1966), p. 209.

[3]*The Knack of Using Your Subconscious Mind* by John K. Williams (Scarsdale, N.Y.: The Updegraff Press, 1952) p. 87.

thought of himself as *the source* of such wisdom as passed his lips; rather, he regarded himself as the go-between—the receiver of a Higher Intelligence which he passed on to those who sought enlightenment from him.

This calls to mind God's promise to the people of Israel that if they obey his moral and civil law—righteous actions—they will be blessed with material abundance. But he warns that this very blessing can serve as a snare. If they forget the real source they will exalt themselves thus: *"My power and the power of mine hand hath gotten me this wealth."* God then promises the inevitable reaction against man's false claim of divinity: "I testify against you this day that ye shall surely perish."[4]

While the Mosaic law in this case refers to material abundance, it is clear that "false claims of divinity" apply no less to the spiritual realm of ideas, insights, intuitive flashes, wisdom, enlightenment. Perish as a result of false claims in this domain? Indeed yes! Have a hard look at the world around us, heading as it is toward disaster. Why? Millions of people are thinking of themselves as *the source* of wisdom and, in consequence, are lording it over others. Rampant authoritarianism!

With Socrates, it is possible for others of us to enter into the realm of the Infinite Unknown. When we do so, there comes a light: Such seeing is experienced, more or less, by all who live, or ever have or will inhabit the earth—except the willfully blind. "None so blind as those who will not see." Not those who *do* not but those who *will* not!

For analogy, imagine 100,000 people in the huge colosseum

---

[4]See *Deuteronomy* 8: 6-20.

on a moonless night. Utter darkness! In the audience are a dozen or so geniuses, scattered here and there—Leonardo, Socrates, Edison, and their rare kind—each of whom lifts a torch. The darkness remains. Now, let each of the 100,000 simultaneously strike a match. Bright as day!

This is how Creation works its wonders when each is *free to pursue his uniqueness.* Over time, countless millions of discoveries, inventions, truths: a teacher of the deaf and the telephone, a grocer and the typesetting machine, a father of an invalid son and the pneumatic tire, an unknown Hindu and the concept of zero. This is the overall luminosity by which we live and prosper. It accounts for that wisdom in the market which is far, far greater than exists in any discrete individual—even a Socrates. Freedom by a recognition of *the* Source—not mine but Thine!

The source? Ralph Waldo Emerson identifies the wellspring as "immense intelligence." We are, he asserts, *"receivers* of its truth and *organs* of its activity." To become seers—beholders of truth and justice—we do no more than allow a passage of its beams. In a word, we allow the "immense intelligence" to flow and intercept as much of it as we can. This is the source, beyond you or me or any other finite being.

When an individual thinks of himself as source—"false claim to divinity"—the source thereby ceases to function and to flow.

This attempt to stop the flow . . . has proved the greatest obstruction in history. It causes war, unending misery and chaos. It is based on the illusion that man in his littleness is all. It assumes that there is no universal power, no God, no Plan. It is man getting in the way, man out of the main stream. There are only two kinds of people, the sick and the well, and the sick are those who block the rhythm of flowing and ascension.[5]

I would conclude with these three thoughts: First, reflect upon the praise, adulation, esteem heaped upon Socrates, Leonardo, Edison, Emerson, and numerous other seers. Inflate their ego? Indeed not! These men were aware of two incontestable facts: (1) that of not being the source; and (2) that taking credit is a "false claim of divinity" which, in turn, switches off the Source, allowing no more passage of its beams, nothing remaining to intercept.

Second, it may be possible for me to see a light; the light cannot see me. I may grasp the enlightenment that was Emerson's; that enlightenment is unaware of my existence. The initiative—in both cases—must be mine. As to the "immense intelligence," I do not know *what* it is, only *that* it is. If this mysterious Intelligence does know of me, I have no way of knowing for certain that it does. Why, then, should I not reach up for it, that is, apprehend what I can of it? "Insight seems to be the voice of the universal power. . . . And it comes only to that mind which consents to be used."[6] By reaching, one consents.

Finally, let each of us look for as much of that light as is within his power to perceive. Be among those who see: seers. Let others who can see more—the Leonardos—do their more, as I do my little. This, in my view, is the prescription for a harmonious society. Insofar as we become seers, freedom reigns!

---

[5]See *Consent* by Newton Dillaway (Unity Village, Mo.: Unity Books, 1967), p. 94.

[6]*Ibid.*, p. 28.

22

BELIEVE THE BEST
OF EVERY MAN

I have believed the best of every man,
And find that to believe it is enough
To make a bad man show him at his best,
Or even a good man swing his lantern higher.

—WILLIAM BUTLER YEATS

Yeats, the 1923 Nobel Prize winner in literature, reveals far more than literary talent; this verse shows a remarkable philosophic and psychologic insight. To believe the best of every man assuredly is among the highest attainments of mortal beings. It is difficult to do because it runs counter to our instincts.

It is easy enough to believe the best of those few we observe and know and automatically classify as "good men." But our very act of judging one man to be "good" leads just as thoughtlessly to the judgment of others as "bad men," of whom no good might be expected.

Take my own case. Do I believe the best of *every* man? Up

until now, no! Can I? The attainment is just this side of
sprouting wings. Is it worth the try? Yes, anything that's
right justifies the effort. And for devotees of the freedom
philosophy, we have here an overlooked formula of enormous
importance. Here is an obstacle which might be likened to a
block of granite. It is, as some thinkers have suggested, an
insurmountable wall in the pathway of the weak but a steppingstone in the pathway of the strong.

We favor the free society, or well we might; we aspire to be
strong and not weak. Let us then examine Yeats' high attainment as a steppingstone.

There are two steps in this "block of granite." The first is
a belief in the best of every man. If we search hard enough,
we may recognize that there is a bit of good even in a thief—
he may be good to his dog. As Joaquin Miller phrased it:

> In men whom men condemn as ill
> I find so much of goodness still.

Is such recognition "enough to make a bad man show him
at his best"? According to Franklin, "There is no Man so Bad
but he secretly respects the Good." And undeniably, we who
search for and call attention to the good in bad men advance
the good in ourselves.

Assess this idea the other way around. You and I, though
aware of faults galore, are disposed to rank ourselves among
the good men. When others call attention to the best in us,
does it not cause us to swing our lanterns higher? I'll wager
it works that way on you as it does on me. We can learn how
others react by simply discovering how we respond. The
message comes through loud and clear.

The second and by far the most difficult step in this "block of granite" is to practice what we believe to be right. It's one thing to know the right but quite another matter to live it. I am acquainted with countless persons whose announced notions are, in my view, ridiculous. Do I overlook their opinions and try to see the best in them? To the contrary, I focus on the worst in them and link the notions to the persons. Alone in this? Hardly! Mine is a confession that might well be made by the vast majority of freedom devotees, and most everyone else.

To dwell on the mistakes or evils I see in others is a degrading activity on my part though I confess to doing it often. Having made the confession, what is next? A personal decision: I hereby resolve to get this malignancy out of me; I shall no longer even think of others as bad and for two reasons: (1) such thinking is bad for me and (2) it does injury to all others who are the objects of this mischief; it accentuates the badness in them!

Does this mean that pernicious notions should go without censure? Of course not! But condemn the deed, not the doer! The formula is this: Think not of the tyrant as a fool, only of the domineering trait as foolish. It has been wisely said, "Hate not the sinner, only the sin." Censure the doer for his deed and he'll defend the deed. But explain the harmful consequences of the deed, that is, divorce the action from the actor and, if he sees why his way is wrong, he will abandon it promptly. No one tries to do poorly.

To illustrate how this approach works, let me cite the story of a friend who found himself unfavorably disposed toward one of his associates. He had been taught not to criticize another for his faults but, rather, to await some action which he could approve and applaud. He waited for six months and then came an action he could sincerely and honestly commend. Friends ever after! This brought out the best in both. Each swung his lantern higher.

Over the years, in the works of numerous famous men, I have found all too many ideas contrary to my way of thinking. But to berate them for this would be utter folly on my part. Instead, I must study their acts and writings for things I can applaud, as in this passage from Arnold Toynbee:

> When man mistakes himself for God, he is sounding the death knell of human freedom. For, when man comes to believe that he is God, he falls to worshipping himself. And when man worships himself, his human idol is not the individual human being: it is the collective power of corporate humanity. . . . The idolization of collective human power turns all the idolaters into slaves.

It is not that my praise of this wise observation will cause Toynbee to swing his lantern higher—he never heard of me. But reflect on the added attention that would be given to this enlightened statement among those in my orbit who are his admirers, or the effect on the celebrated historian himself were this approach used by the great and the near great known to him. All would be to the good, bringing out the best in all—swinging their lanterns higher.

Here, in my judgment, is an important—indeed a necessary step—in winning friends for freedom. In any event, it is a step I am determined to take regardless of the difficulty. Thoreau encourages me: "It is very rare that you meet with obstacles in this world which the humblest man has not the facilities to surmount." In all humility, then, let me attend to my part, the only part in the world for which I am responsible.

23

I LIKE YOU, TOO

It makes all the difference in the world whether we put Truth in the first place or in the second place.
—ARCHBISHOP WHATELEY

Switching from one TV channel to another, I stopped momentarily to audition a debate between a noted socialist and a self-styled conservative. What a confrontation! And to what purpose? It was obvious that neither party moved the other his way. Each came to listen only to himself, and went away more firmly convinced than before. To the viewing audience, this had the value of a prize fight: entertainment. No enlightenment could possibly result from such a hassle, for each contestant rated verbal victory ahead of truth. Each aimed to outwit the other and thus gain applause or perhaps a following.

But let's not judge such wrangling too harshly; most of us are addicted ourselves, and daily indulge in the same thing

small-scale. That is, we lock horns with our ideological op-
posites, and with no more shedding of light than from the
TV performance.

This poses the question: What then? Will not freedom suffer if we drop our combative postures? My answer, having
been learned the hard way, has changed from an insistent
"Yes!" to an emphatic "No!" What follows is the case for a
better way.

Several of us were relaxing at luncheon during a FEE Seminar. A free market affirmation of mine, quite at odds with
popular notions, evoked from a lady, "I *absolutely* disagree with you." My response, "I like you, too," brought a
good-natured chuckle and ended the discussion on that subject for the time being. At the Seminar's conclusion, the lady
waved a smiling farewell, "I like you, too."

It isn't that "I like you, too" is necessarily an appropriate
response to a mind that has suddenly closed; but it symbolizes
a recommended attitude, that is, if the purpose of discussion
is mutual enlightenment. Upgrading understanding has no
greater deterrent than two overly-serious, humorless, closed
minds squared off against each other in verbal combat.
Nothing but ill-feeling can result from such behavior. To open
the door, educationally, one of the two must break the combative spell.

Though it affronts my instincts, *I am done with argument!*
Contentiousness and confrontations demote rather than promote the ideal. And that cuts out a lot of talk! Leave verbal
combativeness to those who naively expect that repulsion will
somehow induce attraction, that intolerance of another will
draw him to you, that displaying a closed mind will inspire
others to explore it, that know-it-all-ness will invite others to

partake of the know-it-all's "knowledge." Might as well expect darkness to give light.

Indeed, I have resolved not to enter upon ideological and philosophical matters with anyone unless that other is seeking light from me or I from him toward which we should forever strive. Such remarks as "I *absolutely* disagree with you," and other variations of intellectual absolutism, can hardly be construed as quests for light.

A logical corollary of this posture requires of me that I never think ill of another for avoiding my light or even for slamming the door in my face. *It's his door.* My only point is that a mind closed to me is the signal for me to stop, or to introduce some disarming humor, or turn the talk to trivia. It is the signal to look elsewhere, to a more fruitful engagement. That bit of discussion is all over—finished!—unless one lets his disappointment overrule his reason and goes on to "spin his wheels," that is, to waste his time and energy.

"But," goes the rejoinder, "were I to confine my ideological talk to those seeking light from me or I from them, I probably wouldn't do any talking at all," the implication being that freedom would thereby suffer. Wrong! Silence is far better than talk that gives offense; further, quietude is preferable to the kind of talk for which there are no ears.

The rule of silence on ideological matters until asked, if faithfully adhered to, would seem at first blush to dispense with nearly all discussions of political economy. Quite the contrary! It is easily demonstrable that invited, much-desired, and appreciated talk can be substituted for that brand of uninvited talk which either offends or falls on deaf ears.

Over and over again we hear the plaint, "I don't have time for the kind of study and reflection that would make me a

competent student and teacher of the freedom philosophy!"
Invariably, these words are from those addicted to argument.
By their own admission they lack competence; yet, they fritter
away a great deal of time in useless if not offensive talk.

Were these persons to shun argument—confrontations—they
would have time galore, enough to stock the mind with better
understanding and a more skillful exposition. As self-
improvement takes place, others begin seeking one's counsel;
as proficiency is achieved, the demand for talk increases.
Countless instances can be cited of a demand too great for
accommodation. And with the doors of perception wide open
—eager listeners!

The rule would seem to be: *Go only where called, but do
everything within one's power to qualify to be called.*

Consider the distinction between talking and writing. Few
of us talk to ourselves; most talk is in the presence of others.
If it is unwanted, there is no genteel means of escape. Offense, in these circumstances, is unavoidable. Writing can be
and often is contentious, but everyone is free not to read it.
And a nonreader can be unattentive without being rude. The
written polemic has an advantage over the spoken, for it
carries no built-in obtrusiveness; it allows freedom of choice.

Exploratory, as distinguished from contentious writing,
paves the way for invited talk. Enlightening writers are much
in demand as speakers.

Further, writing is a stern taskmaster; it permits one to see
with a discerning and skeptical eye what really is in the mind.
Time and again we hear the erroneous notion, "The idea is as
clear as crystal but I can't put it in writing." Unless one ad-
mits having no vocabulary, what cannot be put clearly in
writing is not clear in the mind. Much of the loose ideological

talk we hear is only muddled thinking; it is composed of a mental potpourri, an agglomeration of notions that have not been subjected to refinement by writing. It often happens that a "clear-as-crystal" idea, when committed to paper, is revealed as either fuzzy or false. For improvement, one must return again to the mind for clarification. The thinking-it-through process involved in writing is the genesis of the kind of enlightening talk that is avidly sought and that opens the doors of perception.

Any improving person becomes tolerant of those who hold differing or even opposing views; for he finds that today he doesn't exactly agree with his yesterday's self. Holding no grudge against his earlier unenlightened self, how can he logically think ill of another for not agreeing with his present views? Indeed, the improving person can quite honestly respond to one who *absolutely* disagrees: "I like you, too." And what a boon this attitude would be to the ideal we seek!

24

THE GREATEST GAME
IN LIFE

Now, you cannot go on being a
good egg forever; you must either
hatch or rot.

—C. S. LEWIS

The humorous remark by C. S. Lewis about hatching or rotting was inspired by Heraclitus, the Greek philosopher of twenty-five centuries ago: "Man is on earth as in an egg." While analogies are always a risky means of communication, especially if there is an element of comedy in them, there is, nonetheless, a thought here worth exploring.

Conceded, eggs and human beings are far from comparable. Many eggs are not fertile and, thus, have no chance of hatching; they are destined to be eaten or to rot. Human beings, on the other hand—all of them—have the potentiality of hatching. Again I quote this bit of wisdom by the eminent German psychologist, Fritz Kunkel: "Immense hidden powers lurk in the unconscious of the most common man— indeed, of all people without exception."

What is the generally overlooked feature of the individual that has the potentiality of hatching or the dreadful alternative of rotting—that either blooms or decays? Kunkel gives us the clue: "Hidden powers lurk in the unconscious." That is to say, we possess powers of which we are not normally aware. So, our problem is to become conscious of those powers. The alternative is *stagnation at the unconscious level which, in itself, is rotting.* In a word, it is consciousness that has the potentiality of hatching.

I have arrived at this conclusion by asking some difficult questions and finding answers that seem to square with reality. For instance: What is man's earthly purpose? Is it fame, fortune, political power, popularity, longevity, retirement to a do-nothing status, as so many seem to believe?

To my way of thinking, there is no rational answer to this question—what is man's earthly purpose?—except as our answer is reasoned from a basic premise. My premise or fundamental point of reference is founded on three assumptions:

- Man did not create himself, for it is easily demonstrable that man knows very little about himself. Therefore, my first assumption is the primacy and supremacy of an Infinite Consciousness.

- My second assumption is also demonstrable. While difficult, it is possible for the individual to expand his own awareness, perception, consciousness.

- My third assumption is a profound belief that the intellect—one's mind—is independent; that is to say, it is not subordinate to the organic matter of which one's body is composed. An inference from this belief is a conviction of the immortality of the human spirit or consciousness, this earthly moment not being all there is to it. It is consciousness that is immortalized, not the body or wealth or fame or any such thing. In a word, consciousness is *the* reality!

Conceding the correctness of these assumptions, man's earthly purpose is clear as crystal. It is to see how close one can come during this mortal moment to expanding his consciousness into a harmony with Infinite Consciousness—to see how close one can come to a realization of those aptitudes and potentialities uniquely his own, there being no two of us alike. Summarized, my highest purpose is to develop, grow, emerge, evolve; it is not to stagnate—rot—but rather to hatch!

My rules for hatching may not be the best for you, but I offer these two for what they are worth. First, resolve to begin thinking for self on the more important life issues—individualistic and societal: Start the cerebral machinery; avoid stagnation. Except for mundane matters, an alarming number of people in today's world let others do their thinking for them; they are only imitators and rarely know who to imitate. Certainly, seek the counsel of those considered wiser; but make up one's own mind on all matters pertaining to self and society.

Second, answer the question, what am I here for? In brief, acquire a basic premise. After finding one that satisfies, size up all ideas in its light. If an idea is antagonistic to the premise, reject it. If, on the other hand, it is in harmony with and promotive of the premise, accept and abide by it.

The meaning of "abide by it"? Stand by one's honest convictions "come hell or high water"! This is integrity. But is there not the danger that one might be honestly convinced that he should, for instance, feather his own nest at the expense of others? Not if he is thinking for self, has a sound premise, reasons logically and deductively from it, and abides by his findings. Hatching—expanding the consciousness—exposes more and more of the unknown. The more one knows the more he knows he does not know. Indeed, if one is not daily becoming more and more aware of how little he knows, he is not growing; if humility is not replacing arrogance, he is not hatching.

A bit more on this point. Stagnation is not the curse of mental sluggards only. The cessation of growth or hatching afflicts those with the highest IQ's perhaps more than the mill run of us. The explanation? If one be smarter, more brilliant, than all others observed by him, why go further? Isn't such "superiority" adequate? With the eye cast toward the relative inferiority of others, it is not turned toward the yet-to-know. Stagnation at the high IQ level! Know-it-alls! Here is a useful guideline: Any time an individual is observed whose tendency is to lord it over others, either in the home or public office, draw the accurate conclusion that he has stagnated, regardless of his so-called intelligence quotient, be it high or low!

Any individual who is truly growing in consciousness, be his IQ moderate or high, will grasp the simple fact of self-responsibility and its correlate, freedom. He cannot help seeing that no one can be self-responsible unless free and that no one can be free unless self-responsible. No dictocrats among those who are hatching!

Now to the importance of individual hatching as related to society. One cannot imagine a good society composed only of persons at the stagnation stage. On what does a good society depend? On a natural aristocracy! Who are these aristocrats? Only those who are growing in consciousness—hatching!

Said Thomas Jefferson, "There is a natural aristocracy among men; it is composed of virtues and talents." Inane or silly notions in the heads of men are no more numerous today than a century ago. Why are they more in evidence now than then? When the natural aristocracy is in the pink of condition, such notions are held in abeyance; people do not like to make fools of themselves before exemplars, those for whom there is a high respect. But when this natural aristocracy is in a slump, as today, these notions have little if anything standing against them. If it is all right for leaders in business, labor, politics, religion, education not to heed integrity and the other virtues, why not all right for everyone?

The exemplars, those who set high standards of conduct are, at best, few in number, on occasion nearly extinct. If the U.S.A. is to move again in the right direction, a natural aristocracy has to be reborn. Definitely, this is not a numbers but a quality problem. Where must one seek this quality? From that individual—man or woman—viewed in the mirror; look not elsewhere!

True, hatching must be the objective of the individual for his own sake—the eye focused on the growth of one's own consciousness, not the reforming of others. My hatching can only be achieved in me and by me. Self-interest, however, inspires the hope that others will also grow in consciousness at a pace even faster than one's own. Why? Being surrounded by persons in a state of stagnation depresses rather than encourages personal achievement. On the other hand, superior exemplars—aristocrats of the highest order—create a magnetic field toward which one is drawn. Exemplars are one's benefactors.

What to do? Try one's best and hope for the best; outdistance everyone you possibly can, and hope that others will outdistance you. Make hatching a game of leapfrog—the greatest game in life!

25

WHO IS A TEACHER?

There is not enough darkness in the whole world to put out the light of one wee candle.

—A SCOTTISH EPITAPH

We are pursuing Truth when searching for a Teacher; we stray far from it when promoting ourselves as teachers.

Here, I am trying to deal with two different roles in life. One is often mistaken for the other, so let us mark the distinction between them by using "teacher" and Teacher! The first is what millions of classroom instructors call themselves; the second is a tribute one person pays to another. The former demands, more often than not, that you listen to him; the latter is well aware that the student listens only to those he thinks will enlighten him.

I emphasized the idea of Teacher in a brief eulogy to Ludwig von Mises at the Memorial Service for him on October 16, 1973:

"The proudest tribute mankind pays to one it would most

150

honor is to call him Teacher. The man who releases an idea which helps men understand themselves and the universe puts mankind forever in his debt. In whatever directions progress is possible, the Teacher is one who has moved out ahead of inquiring humanity and by the sheer power of ideas has drawn men toward him. Men would stagnate otherwise. Historians may label an age for some ruler, such as the age of Charlemagne or Louis XIV, but the true Teacher is not for an age; he is for all time.

"Ludwig Mises is truly—and I use this in the present tense—a Teacher. More than two generations have studied under him and countless thousands of others have learned from his books. Books and students are the enduring monuments of a Teacher and these monuments are his. This generation of students will pass away but the ideas set in motion by his writings will be a fountain source for new students for countless generations to come.

"We have learned far more from Ludwig Mises than economics. We have come to know an exemplar of scholarship, a veritable giant of erudition, steadfastness, and dedication. Truly one of the great Teachers of all time! And so, all of us salute you, Ludwig Mises, as you depart this mortal life and join the immortals."

For well over half a century thousands of students in Europe and America entered classrooms that they might learn from this great Teacher. Yet, never in the 32 years of our intimate acquaintance did I ever hear him refer to himself as a "teacher." Indeed, he was continuously seeking light, as were those who came to share his wisdom.

"There is not enough darkness in the whole world to put out the light of one wee candle." To overlook this simple fact leads to discouragement and disaster. Therefore, it is important to realize that ignorance gives way to enlightenment precisely as darkness recedes when light is increased. Ignorance? In technology, no; knowledge in this area has increased fantastically. However, in matters of political economy, ignorance appears to be gaining until it seems overwhelming, unbeatable. Reflect on these words of another outstanding Teacher, W. A. Paton, Professor Emeritus of Accounting and of Economics, University of Michigan:

"Although the only form of life on the planet capable of careful scrutiny and pondering with respect to himself and his surroundings, Homo sapiens has often proved to be an easy mark for the witch doctor, the soothsayer, the spellbinder, and other nonsense peddlers. But I doubt if at any earlier period were people generally so susceptible to economic pipe dreams and pie-in-the-sky proposals as we are today. If we don't go beyond American history the case is clear.

"Our forefathers, at no stage, would have widely accepted the view that the road to prosperity, the abundant life for all, is by way of blocking early entry to the working ranks, an enforced 40-hour—or less—work week, with the trimmings of minimum wage laws, paid vacations, featherbedding and soldiering, and retirement with a handsome pension after 30 years of service, coupled with a program of government handouts on a vast scale to those unemployed for almost any reason or excuse. They were addicted to hard work, recognized that we can't consume what we don't produce, and were skeptical of all schemes to pick ourselves up by our bootstraps. And they would be shocked by today's widespread tide of vandalism, violence, and disorder, which is becoming a serious obstacle to efficient utilization of available resources and increasing—or even maintaining—the level of economic output.

"It should also be noted that the astrologers, fortunetellers, seers, gurus, ESP experts, and assorted cult leaders—as well as the economic con men—are flourishing these days."

So it *is* dark! Hopeless? Of course not! But we need to re-examine the methods of freedom, whose devotees, all too often, stumble aimlessly in the authoritarian darkness that pervades the face of the earth. The solution? Set the method straight, that is, switch from "teacher" to Teacher. There are two guidelines which, if scrupulously observed, will lead toward freedom.

Better, not bitter! "It is better to light a candle than to curse the darkness." Cursing the darkness is harmful, not helpful. Not only does this tactic fail to dispel the prevailing darkness but, worse, it darkens and literally poisons the soul of anyone who so indulges, as most M.D.'s will attest. Be done with bitterness! What then? Accept the fact that neither you nor anyone else has gone very far in understanding the freedom philosophy and explaining it clearly. Frankly, all of us are babes in the woods. The best any of us can do is to concentrate on achieving maturity, on becoming better. Not only is this procedure joyous and psychologically sound but, to the extent it succeeds, to that extent is light increased and darkness dispelled.

Look up, not down. Few, indeed, are those who resist the powerful and nonrational tendency to look down upon others who are thought to be lacking in wisdom. By downgrading others, the individual stares into the darkness and, with his eyes thus cast, becomes a "teacher." "Listen to me," he shouts, a message for which there are no ears to hear or eyes to see. A broadcaster, but no receiving sets; a broad-caster who has closed his mind to the enlightenment which could be his if he were to raise his sights, rather than lower them!

Look up to what—or to whom? Look to the Teacher! Probe all mankind, past and present, for those who are wiser than self. Wherever you stand in the scale of wisdom, the Teacher is not difficult to find. Forever look upward and listen; become a receiving set. Truth arises from strange, varied, and unsuspected sources and is revealed exclusively to seekers. "None are so blind as those who will not see."

Again, that bit of wisdom: "There is not enough darkness in the whole world to put out the light of one wee candle." If I succeed in lighting my wee candle from my chosen Teacher—and others do the same—then we multiply the number of Teachers; darkness, having no resistance to light, will gradually and surely recede. Enlightenment comes in no other way, but invariably comes if we follow correct method!

26

THE RARE MOMENT

The rare moment is not the mo-
ment when there is something
worth looking at, but the moment
when we are capable of seeing.
—JOSEPH WOOD KRUTCH

When *is* there "something worth looking at"? Any time!
There are good things to see at all times, in all places, and by
all individuals. It's a matter of personal choice; and how
varied are these value judgments of individuals! For instance,
there are many who are more attracted to the labor-saving device known as thievery than to anything else. They think
stealing is a procedure "worth looking at."

Pause here for a moment. Some of us think of thievery—
whether carried out by individuals or practiced collectively
"from each according to ability, to each according to need"—
as very low on the scale of values. Why? Simply because our
judgments differ from, and are presumed to be at a higher
level than, those of the thief. But we must be careful in con-
demning persons whose value judgments are, in our opinion,
lower than our own. For implicit in such an attitude is the

claim that we are superior. After all, who is any of us but an imperfect mortal! If we demand that others see things as we do, we are opening the door to the possibility that we should be forced to look at only what a governing majority of others believe to be worth looking at. And bear in mind that no two of us have the same judgments; indeed, one's own values change from one day to the next. So, we need the flexibility to cope with constant changes. I would let each decide for himself what's worth looking at and suffer the penalties of his errors or the blessings of his righteousness.

Man's ideas as to what's worth looking at range from pornography to sunsets; from Picasso to Raphael; from the Pyramids to the Jungfrau; from ancient ruins to the Taj Mahal; from *Soviet Life* to the Holy Bible; from atoms to galaxies; from Bach to rock. Ideas and ambitions range from state socialism to individual liberty; from a square meal to an elaborate symphony; from quiet repose to strenuous executive activity; from a decent burial to a voyage of exploration over uncharted seas; from the cheapest fiction to the purest science or philosophy; from thinking for self to imitating others—you name it!

Krutch is right. The rare moment is not the moment when there is something worth looking at. What could be more common? Every moment of one's life affords that opportunity.

The rare moment is when we are capable of seeing—that rare glimpse into the mystery of that which is observed. Most people only look at a flash of lightning; they see nothing of its miraculous nature. While no one knows what it is, there have been a few who see beyond what meets the eye; they have seen enough to generate and harness electricity to our use. This kind of seeing—insight—occurs only in the rarest of moments.

Many of us look at a sunset and are overcome by its beauty. How few of us, even today, perceive that the sun does not set? Many see no more than was seen by the first man on earth. How many, before or since Copernicus, have understood that the setting of the sun is an illusion, rather that the earth is rotating? Rare moments, indeed.

Another example of a rare moment: Ever since man first set foot in Switzerland, that majestic mountain, the Jungfrau, has ranked high among the beauties of nature, truly worth looking at. People by untold thousands have stood at its base looking up in awe. Around the turn of the century an entrepreneur had a vision, a moment of seeing: Why not multiply what's worth looking at? Make it possible for the thousands to go atop the Jungfrau that they might see the beauty from that vantage point! Some twelve miles of tunnel was bored through the rock, a cog railroad installed, and a wonderful hostelry built within the mountain near the top. Private enterprise! No government subsidy! Just one of those rare moments of seeing which is more in evidence when man is free and self-responsible.

Near the top of the list of things thought to be worth looking at is wealth—material affluence. The aggregate of the moments spent in seeking wealth staggers the imagination. But note how rare the moments when individuals are capable of seeing the preconditions for gaining affluence; a society of free and self-responsible individuals with government limited to codifying and inhibiting destructive actions. If government thus performs, people are free to act creatively as they please. And there is no other way to material well-being.

Not seeing for themselves, the masses listen to false prophets, persons who promise that we can spend ourselves rich, that prosperity derives from dictatorial control over wages, hours of labor, exchanges, prices, and so on. They hear the promises but cannot foresee the consequences of the methods to be used.

Wrote Ralph Barton Perry: "Ignorance deprives men of freedom because they do not know what alternatives there are."

An affluent society cannot prevail unless individuals see that their economic well-being stems from the general practice of the principles of private ownership, the free market, and limited government.

Perhaps the power to run the lives of others tops the list of things a majority believe to be worth looking at. Rare, indeed, are the moments when these individuals are capable of seeing the futility of their way. Were I the wisest philosopher or politician who ever lived, there is not one of these meddlers who believes I could run his life better than he. But he, unwise, has no doubt about his powers to run your life and mine. Why unwise? The very first step in wisdom is an awareness of how little one knows. Nor do such people see that power corrupts them!

Most of us doubtless have the potential to see ever so much more than we customarily perceive. We rarely see more than we wish to see. As unique individuals, we tend to specialize, to focus on the details from a particular point of view. Such focusing gives us more intimate knowledge of the tree, the trunk, the root, the twig, the leaf, the miracle within the single cell. I have my special interest, you yours, things we see more clearly, while neglecting many other possible vistas. The danger of too narrow a specialization is that we can't see the forest for the trees.

The "forest" worth looking at which most intrigues me is a viable society, one featured by harmonious relationships, one in which the individual may proceed, unobstructed by others toward a realization of his creative aptitudes and potentialities. If a person fails to overcome his own obstacles—frustrations, superstitions, imperfections, ignorance, no will to strive —that's his problem. But if the obstacles are put there by others—if the individual is compelled to live as others dictate —that is everyone's problem. Freedom is everyone's business!

Why is freedom everyone's business? It is because my freedom depends on yours and vice versa. There is but faint appreciation of the high degree of specialization in contemporary society, of how dependent each of us is on the others. In short, we are now interdependent beyond recall; there is no turning back. This is to say that we, in our age, are at once *social* and individualistic beings. And if we fail or refuse to recognize this fact, all will fall together.

Of course, the individualistic side of this coin—being one's best self—is a problem of the first magnitude. Each of us must wrestle with this personally. Many, I suspect, see this. It is the social side of the coin they fail to see. How can ordinary mortals, such as you and I, fulfill this aspect of life? The formula is simple. Never do unto others that which you would not have them do unto you. If you wouldn't have others control your life, then never try to control anyone else. If you wouldn't have others hinder you from producing, freely exchanging, owning the fruits of your own labor, competing, traveling, then don't inhibit these practices among your fellowmen. This is all one has to do to fulfill his role as a social being. Merely heed the oldest, wisest, and simplest maxim ever written!

Finally, is there a prescription for removing our blindfolds? Is there a mode of conduct or discipline which would open up new vistas, permitting you and me to see more than we now do? I am just beginning to see that the answer is *integrity*.

For years, I have been defining integrity as the accurate reflection in *word* and *deed* of whatever one's highest conscience dictates as right. This may not in fact be right but it is as close to righteousness as one can get.

My definition stands; but I see now that my preachments—words—have been better arranged than my practice—deeds. It is my practice of integrity that must be improved.

To illustrate this failing on my part: I have written that each of us should await discovery, that if there is anything in our garden worth looking at, it will be detected by others.[1] Do I heed this? Only with the greatest difficulty! Impatience tends to govern me, more or less. I can hardly wait till others find out how good I think I am at this or that. This nagging urge is a common trait and accounts, in no small measure, for the urge to reform that plagues humanity. Out of such a garden grows nothing but weeds. When I cannot believe and abide by my own admonitions, am I to expect better of others! Seeing and doing must become one and the same. To see the right without doing it is to live without integrity.

Why is it that integrity removes the blindfolds, improves seeing? Some of the reasons are apparent.

I repeat, while one's accurate reflections in word and deed may not in fact be truth, they are as close to truth as one can

---

[1] See the chapter, "Await Discovery," in *Having My Way* (Irvington-on-Hudson, N.Y.: Foundation for Economic Education, Inc., 1974) pp. 40-44.

get. Even though we err, our devotion to integrity leads toward that which is right; this is the only road to truth. Those truth seekers who practice integrity themselves are drawn to integrity in others. This virtue has a magnetic quality. Are not the persons to whom you listen those who manifest integrity?

When others are being drawn toward your honest reflections, your light tends to brighten. Their attention is an encouragement, a stimulant, to put your best foot forward. In a word, integrity works its attractions back and forth among us; and the rare moment becomes a more common experience. Wrote Charles Simmons:

Integrity is the first step to true greatness. Men love to praise [it], but are slow to practice it. To maintain it in high places costs self-denial; in all places it is liable to opposition; but its end is glorious, and the universe will yet do it homage.

27

STILL MORE TO DO?

*Do every creative thing possible
in this life.*

These comments have to do with age, which tends to reveal mine. I was 12 years old when Halley's Comet last flashed across the sky. Will I see that marvel of the heavens a second time? Possibly, if I can still see! However, that is not the relevant question. Rather, it is this: Whatever years remain of this mortal life, am I warranted in letting up? Is there still more for me to do? Indeed, yes—until the last moment!

No two persons share identical ideas concerning what comes after earthly existence. Guesses range all the way from nothing, to hell and damnation, to countless forms of heavenly bliss. Thus, little if anything is to be gained by intruding my speculations into this hodge-podge of after-life expectations and hopes. As with many others, the future is not known to me.

There is, however, one view to which I hold firm: the immortality of the human spirit or consciousness. For it is clearly evident that every individual, to some extent, leaves traces of his existence, be it noble or ignoble, forever and ever, and that all humanity thenceforth is moved this way or that as a consequence. As "every heartbeat is felt through the entire universe," so is every action of yours or mine felt by all who live now and ever after. In this sense, if in no other, we are immortal. It is this idea of immortality I wish to explore.

By and large, people fail to appreciate the enduring significance of their own lives. So far as future generations are concerned, they have little if any feeling of relatedness; their concern is limited to themselves or to the few contemporaries they find within their tiny orbits. They do not recognize themselves as integral components of a flowing process—of the future influenced and more or less shaped by what they are and do today. Unaware of their immortality, they fail to live up to the best of their lives.

The definition of immortal to which I refer is "lasting as long as this world; enduring." What lasts? What is enduring? It is you, regardless of what you reflect, be it truth or untruth, good or bad, virtue or evil, moral or immoral. In a word, it is you and your actions in this life.

Let me cite a couple of examples. First, an extremely powerful authoritarian: Adolf Hitler. That power-drunk character left a scar, a blight that never will be erased from humanity. Mankind will forever feel the effects of the malady he spearheaded. Hitler, no less than anyone else, is immortal. He polluted the human stream and the debris flows on and on.

Second, reflect on a man most everyone would think of as a nobody, a Roman slave of nearly 2,000 years ago. This man was exiled because he expressed ideas contrary to Emperor Domitian's political establishment. The exiled slave went to Nicopolis, a small village in northwest Greece, setting up his own school. Students came from Athens and Rome. While he did no writing, his thoughts were recorded—so enlightening that they mirrored their way through fifteen, sixteen, and seventeen centuries and had enormous influence on such noted philosophers as Montaigne, Grotius, Descartes, Pascal, Montesquieu, Adam Smith, Adam Ferguson, Kant, and others. Immortality of a high order is accorded the slave, Epictetus.

As is true of all mortals—including the Hitler variety—their impact may dim over the ages, but bear in mind that there is no fraction so small that it is not still divisible. Everyone, regardless of race, creed, color, education, or religion contributes to the shaping of humanity now and forever.

Perhaps a good way to highlight my point is to imagine yourself as the sole style setter for all future generations—just you and no one else. This would put the responsibility for mankind's future squarely on your shoulders. Would this not change your life, make you strive to achieve immortality of the highest quality? Would not your every act, thought, utterance, behavior be as near to perfection as you could possibly make it? It could not be otherwise!

In reality, however, it is not just you and no one else but, rather, every living human being whose earthly life is immortal! That you are but one among billions, is no logical reason to shift emphasis. Why should not high-grade immortality be as much your goal in the real world of men and nations as if the role of exemplar of mankind were yours alone? The proper role of the individual is not changed by the fact that he is only one among the billions who comprise human society in 1975.

So, why is it that I am not warranted in letting up, calling it quits, regardless of age? Why must I strive right up to the last moment?

My answer: Man is by nature imperfect. Thus, the perfect exemplar is never to be expected, only approximated, and each person contributes his little bit. High quality immortality requires probing, inching ahead, using every moment one is given—including the last one!

28

FAITH WORKS MIRACLES

Miracle is the darling child of faith.
—GOETHE

What is a miracle? It is, says the dictionary, "an event or action that apparently contradicts *known* scientific laws." The question I wish to examine: Is Liberty a miracle? My answer is yes, for Liberty is not verifiable by any *known* scientific laws, indeed, it may well contradict such laws.

Tocqueville wrote, "Despotism may govern without faith, but Liberty cannot." If he be right, and I believe he is, then we devotees of Liberty have no way of achieving our goal except by a growing awareness of faith's role in our aspiration.

Faith is believing, and believing works wonders. Believing produces miracles for which there are only the vaguest of explanations. It is not that anything and everything will happen simply because of a belief that it will; not at all! But, within the realm of the possible, how do we increase the prob-

166

ability of achieving the results we seek? We tip the balance in our favor if our efforts are supported by a confident belief that we will succeed. Of course, there isn't a one of us who knows what the possible is; however, we are constantly expanding its boundaries. But there are limits. A belief that one will never depart this mortal life is demonstrably impossible; there is a record to prove the contrary. Mouthing a belief in spite of contrary evidence is credulity, and credulity is not what we are talking about. Gullibility is the corruption of belief. There is, however, an enormous and unknown realm of the possible in which believing works its wonders.

Being one who subscribes to the powers of faith, let me descend to the mundane—the game of golf—for illustrations.

It was on the 16th green. I was the only one in our foursome who had a chance to win the big event. The sandtrap shot came to rest 25 feet from the cup—all uphill. As always, I addressed the ball, believing that I could sink it, and my putt went straight for the cup—but stopped dead six inches short. And then, as if an unseen hand were at work, it began to roll uphill and into the cup it went! An optical illusion? Had no one else seen this miracle, that is what I would have called it. But my three companions and the two caddies exclaimed in unison, "That ball had stopped!"

When I told of this experience to another later on, he retorted in disbelief, "That defies the law of gravitation." My response, "There are laws and forces at work in this universe that no one knows anything about." A few know *that* there are but not *what* they are.

On another occasion, I did a round of golf with my pro for some instruction. I took note of his almost perfect putting, long putts going to the lip of the cup but never in. On the 13th I said, "Bill, I came here for you to instruct me, but now I have some advice for you. Do you know why those putts don't drop? You don't believe they will. Let me demonstrate." I tossed a ball 30 feet from the cup and stroked it toward the pin. In it went! Two weeks later Bill played the country's most difficult course and never missed a putt under 15 feet. Further, he came within one stroke of tying the course record.

I have made similar demonstrations to others on countless occasions. Show me two golfers of equal physical skill, one of whom believes he can, the other being a doubter. The believer will always excel.

Explain, if you will, why a golfer of my incompetence has had five holes-in-one. Does this faith in results work every time? Of course not! Nonetheless, the results are far better than they would have been were I a doubter—fearing failure as so many do.

While easier said than done, I try to have faith in all walks of life, be it business, health, or whatever. As to business, the German poet, Schlegel, wrote: "In actual life every great enterprise begins with and takes its first forward step in faith."

So far as my business—FEE—is concerned, we have never solicited money from anyone any more than from you, whoever you are. On what then is our financial solvency founded? Faith, pure and simple! It is this: If what we are doing is needed; if we do our work with absolute integrity, never shading a word or phrase for expediency; and if our efforts are reasonably intelligent, then funds will be forthcoming— from whom or whence we know not, but they will come! We have a 29-year record to prove the efficacy of such faith.

As to health, a substantial fraction of the medical profession is convinced that most illness is psychosomatic in origin: fear, stress, anger, doubt, despair—in a word, disbelief.[1]

Good health, on the other hand, is largely the manifestation of a well-conditioned psyche. Observe the mental and physical fitness of the several million people whose prescription for good health is faith—belief that they will have it. "For as he thinketh in his heart, so is he."

I have had countless other experiences that attest to the efficacy of faith. Observers who have had no such experience are prone to ascribe the results to "good luck." Not so! Every seen effect has a cause, often unseen.

A greater error, however, is for the practitioner of faith to ascribe the results to his own genius. Again, not so! Actually, we know not what goes on here except that something does. It is a phenomenon, as mysterious as it is miraculous. Repeated is a possible clue by Emerson:

> We lie in the lap of immense intelligence, which makes us receivers of its truth and organs of its activity. When we discern justice, when we discern truth, *we do nothing of ourselves, but allow a passage of its beams.*

How "allow a passage of its beams"? I suspect the answer is faith. It seems reasonable that no beams of the "immense intelligence" can possibly pass through such blockages as fear, doubt, disbelief. These are nonconductors, obstacles. And belief removes them. By believing, the individual becomes a conductor of this radiant energy. The beams pass through one as naturally as an electric current passes through a copper wire. Without doing anything of ourselves, some of

---

[1] *Man's Presumptuous Brain* by A. T. W. Simeons, M.D. (New York: E. P. Dutton & Co., Inc., 1962).

the beams are intercepted—they become a part of our being.

Now, to the object of our concern: Liberty. There are count-less thousands in America today who believe in Liberty as reverently as I do. But so pronounced is the plunge into state interventionism and welfarism—the very opposite of Lib-erty—that few among our substantial number believe we have a chance. Disbelief! No faith! And short of a switch from doubt and fear to a faith that we can achieve our end, there cannot possibly be a turnabout from authoritarianism to Lib-erty; the case is over, at least for our time.

Reflect on the trillions of people who have inhabited this earth over the ages. Liberty, as we define it, could be likened to the momentary appearance of a bright star in an otherwise dark firmament. Thus, I must think of Liberty as a miracle.

As it is now, our opponents are saying of us, "They have given up; we win." What would they say were a goodly num-ber of us to become believers? Just this: "Those men and women won't down." That in itself would be a miracle. Faith does work miracles—and you'd best believe it.

INDEX

Prepared by Vernelia A. Crawford

The letter "n" following a figure refers to a footnote.

171